A Place in the Sun
SPAIN

Books

WWW.BOOKSATTRANSWORLD.CO.UK

TRANSWORLD PUBLISHERS
61-63 Uxbridge Road, London W5 5SA
a division of The Random House Group Ltd

RANDOM HOUSE AUSTRALIA (PTY) LTD
20 Alfred Street, Milsons Point, Sydney, New South Wales 2061, Australia

RANDOM HOUSE NEW ZEALAND LTD
18 Poland Road, Glenfield, Auckland 10, New Zealand

RANDOM HOUSE SOUTH AFRICA (PTY) LTD
Isle of Houghton, Corner of Boundary and Carse O'Gowrie Roads, Houghton 2198, South Africa

Published 2006 by Channel 4 Books, a division of Transworld Publishers

This book accompanies the television series *A Place in the Sun* made by Freeform Productions for Channel 4

Produced and packaged by Brooklands Communications,
Westgate, 120-128 Station Rd, Redhill, Surrey, RH1 1ET   www.brooklandsgroup.com
Editorial Director: Ann Wallace   Commissioning Editor: Sarah Monaghan
Brooklands would like to thank Manuel Florez-Valcarcel, Notary and Licenciate in Spanish Law
copyright © Brooklands Group Ltd 2006

A catalogue record for this book is available from the British Library.
ISBN 1905026064/ 9781905026067

Printed in Scotland by Scotprint

1 3 5 7 9 10 8 6 4 2

Papers used by Transworld Publishers are natural, recyclable products made
from wood grown in sustainable forests. The manufacturing processes conform
to the environmental regulations of the country of origin.

All pictures courtesy of Pictures Colour Library, except Getty Images front cover and page 76,
David Weston back cover, Richard Parsons pages 32 to 37, Clive Bozzard-Hill page 8, Costa Dorada
Tourism pages 26, 27, 28 and 30 and Spanish Tourist Office pages 38, 40, 42, 44, 45, 47 and 48.

Contributing Authors

Sarah Monaghan

Sarah Monaghan is a true Hispanophile, having lived and studied in Segovia, where she became a fluent Spanish speaker. Currently working as a freelance journalist, Sarah was launch editor of *A Place in the Sun's everything Spain* magazine and her career has included stints in Dubai as editor of consumer lifestyle magazines.

Gordon Miller

Gordon Miller is a freelance journalist who specialises in the overseas property market. He combines a real love of Spain and its culture with a cool business head, and is a frequent contributor to the *A Place in the Sun* group of magazines and the *Independent*.

Richard Way

Richard Way grew up with a second home in the north-east of Spain and has a deep affiliation with the country and its culture. Before becoming editor of *A Place in the Sun's everything Spain* magazine he worked in trade journalism and taught English in Peru, where he learnt Spanish.

Christopher Nye

Christopher Nye was a freelance feature writer for the *Mail on Sunday* and the *Daily Telegraph* before concentrating full-time on the country he loves best for *A Place in the Sun's everything Spain* magazine. He is slowly saving up for a holiday cottage in Asturias.

CONTENTS

FOREWORD

Amanda Lamb may find herself jetsetting all over the world for *A Place in the Sun* but Spain is one of her favourite places to go. Every visit, she discovers something new.

Welcome to the latest title in the *A Place in the Sun* book series. This time we're focusing on Spain, a country that needs little introduction. Over the past 40 years it has proved itself to be of enduring appeal to visitors and property-buyers alike. With ever-expanding low-cost flight options, it's now incredibly easy to get to, and accessible from every corner of the UK.

I first visited Spain with the programme and I have to admit I went with a few preconceptions. I had package holidays and high-rise apartments in my head – but I couldn't have been more wrong. Yes, of course, you can still buy a kiss-me-quick hat and lie on a crowded beach if that's what you want, but Spain boasts such a variety of scenery and cities that it has *so* much more to offer.

My favourite place has to be Tarifa on the Costa de la Luz; in fact, I'm spellbound by the whole Atlantic coastline. I love the big wide expanses of space and the vast, empty, unspoiled beaches with waves rolling in – that's my kind of beach!

Another revelation for me was the warmth and openness of the Spanish people. I've seen them prove their enthusiasm for life time and time again. If you have the chance to attend a local fiesta, jump at it. There's no better way to meet the Spanish and see them at their most relaxed.

If you've picked up this book with the idea of buying in Spain, you'll find it packed with information and answers to a lot of the questions you need to ask. *Where* in Spain do you want to live? Our guides to each region, with tips and interviews with people living there, will help you decide. *How* do you buy in Spain? We've devoted a chapter to the buying process in all its detail: how to raise the money, navigate the purchase procedure, find a solicitor and more. *What* is it like once you're living there? Two further chapters bring you all you need to know about the nuts and bolts of living and working in Spain.

Armed with this book, you can make your Spanish dream come true!

Bay of Biscay

Santander

Bilbao

Santiago de Compostela

Oviedo

Orense

Burgos

Segovia

Salamanca

MADRID

Atlantic

P O R T U G A L

Cáceres

EXTREMADURA

Toledo

Badajoz

ANDALUSIA

Huelva

Seville

Córdoba

Granada

Costa de la Luz

Málaga

Almería

Costa del Sol

Costa de Almería

Cádiz

Ocean

Gibraltar

FRANCE

PYRENEES

SPAIN

Barcelona

Costa Brava

Costa Dorada

Costa del Azahar

Castellón de la Plana

...lencia

Alicante

Costa Blanca

...rcia

...a Cálida

MALLORCA

MENORCA

Palma

IBIZA

Ibiza

FORMENTERA

BALEARIC ISLANDS

Mediterranean Sea

CANARY ISLANDS

La Palma

La Gomera

El Hierro

Tenerife

Santa Cruz

Gran Canaria

Lanzarote

Fuerteventura

ATLANTIC OCEAN

WHY SPAIN?

That's easy! Of all the countries in the world, Spain is still the British nation's favourite destination for both holidaying and buying overseas property.

An astounding half a million of us own a home in Spain, while a quarter of a million British citizens are now registered as official residents – more than in any other European country.

So what is it that attracts us to the land of flamenco and paella? There are many answers to this question but top of the list has to be the weather. Despite Spain being a huge country where the climate changes from region to region, its coastal hot spots, such as the Costa del Sol, guarantee year-round sunshine. Other parts – the Costa Cálida and Costa de Almería, for example – are known not just for warm weather, but also for offering one of the healthiest climates anywhere in the world!

They say that living in the sun makes for a happy, relaxed temperament, and nowhere is this more true than in Spain. Not surprisingly, the laid-back, fun-loving way of life is a huge draw for Brits. But it's a healthy lifestyle, too, encompassing everything from watersports on the glorious beaches along the coast to trekking and riding in the interior and skiing in the Pyrenees and Sierra Nevada.

While Spain's rich and fascinating history is evident in its present-day culture and architecture, modern-day Spain is a wealthy, up-to-the-minute country on a par with any of its European counterparts. It's a key member of the EU and has a solid infrastructure: the Spanish health service is frequently rated as one of the best in Europe, and its transport system has undergone huge improvements in recent years – a government initiative aims to make no city more than a four-hour train journey from Madrid by 2007. The Spanish state education system caters for overseas children and offers the perfect environment for British pupils to grow up bilingual.

It's easy to see how once you get a taste of Spain and its fabulous lifestyle, you'll want to own your own little piece of it. The good news is that the Spanish property market is well established and has something to suit everyone. Getting to Spain from the UK has never been easier: numerous budget airlines operate services between regional airports in Spain and the UK, making weekends away a real possibility.

This improved access to the sun has had a positive effect on Spain's property market. Prices have been rising for the past ten years – last year faster even than in the UK – so buying property is generally a good long-term investment. From glitzy golf apartments and luxury villas, to secluded inland farms and mountain retreats, you're sure to find your dream home.

WHERE IN SPAIN?

Spain is arguably the most geographically diverse country in Europe and is twice the size of the UK, so there's plenty to choose from. Here's our guide.

Spain covers 500,000 square kilometres and is divided into 17 political regions, each with its own unique landscape and personality. The country's northern frontier is marked by the awesome Pyrenees, which form a natural border with France and continental Europe, while in the sun-baked south, Africa blinks at you across the sea, so close you feel you could touch it.

Most of us are familiar with only one Spanish landscape – the Mediterranean coast. This starts in the north-east with the Costa Brava, which runs south from the French border to Barcelona. Its rocky coastline hides beautiful bays with sandy beaches, and highlights include the medieval city of Girona, and the resorts of Tossa de Mar and Blanes.

South of Barcelona lies the Costa Dorada. A favourite with the Spanish and less rugged than its northern neighbour, its notable sights are the pretty resorts of Sitges, Cambrils and Salou, the city of Tarragona – a UNESCO World Heritage Site – and the vast wetlands of the Ebro Delta, an important bird-breeding area.

The Costa del Azahar starts at the Ebro and runs south as far as Oliva, taking in the chic city of Valencia. Sandy beaches are fringed by orange groves and shadowed by the low mountains that run along the coast here. The cape at Jávea, just after Dénia, marks the beginning of the Costa Blanca, one of Spain's two most popular stretches of coast. Benidorm, with its wall of beachside hotels, caters for everything and everyone and, like the nearby smaller resorts of Calpe and Altea, has fantastic, broad beaches.

Left A cove at Formentor, Mallorca

Above The unmistakable spires of Gaudí's architectural masterpiece, the Sagrada Família, in Barcelona

Following page Lush countryside in the Serranía de Ronda, Andalusia

After Alicante, with its busy seafront, you reach Europe's largest saltwater lagoon, the Mar Menor. This is the start of the Costa Cálida, where Mazarrón and Águilas are the major resorts. The coastline becomes more rocky and barren as you hit the Costa de Almería at Vera – the arid landscape made it a favourite shooting ground for spaghetti westerns during the 1960s. There are some beautiful isolated beaches, whilst pretty Mojácar is the area's most-visited town. West from Almería city, the majestic Sierra Nevada mountains loom. The lush foothills and valleys nestling below are known as the Alpujarras, a walkers' and wildlife enthusiasts' heaven.

Back on the coast, the second of Spain's busiest tourist regions, the Costa del Sol, starts to gain momentum at Nerja. Benalmádena, Torremolinos, Fuengirola, Marbella and Puerto Banús have all helped earn it the nickname 'California of Europe'. Away from the beaches, stunning scenery is peppered with whitewashed towns such as Mijas, Ronda, Coín and the Moorish city of Granada.

"Spain's northern frontier is marked by the awesome Pyrenees while in the sun-baked south, Africa blinks at you across the sea, so close you could almost touch it"

The Costa del Sol ends at Gibraltar, and one of Spain's two stretches of Atlantic coastline takes over – the wild, windswept Costa de la Luz. Famous for its windsurfing and vast white beaches, highlights include the towns of Tarifa, Conil de la Frontera, Jerez de la Frontera and the city of Cádiz. Spain's second stretch of Atlantic coast, the Costa Verde, is reminiscent of Cornwall, with ancient fishing villages and sandy bays between craggy headlands. Popular resorts here are Gijón, Llanes, Santillana del Mar and the captivating city of Santander. Finally, you reach the Basque Country and the cities of Bilbao and San Sebastián, in the shadow of the Pyrenees.

In contrast to its bustling coasts, inland Spain remains largely untouched. The landlocked regions of Extremadura and Castilla La Mancha harbour some of Spain's most important historic cities, including Mérida, Trujillo, Guadalupe and Toledo. At the core of Spain's interior is Madrid, a modern, historical and colourful city. Famous for its nightlife, football, architecture and culture, Madrid is as good as a capital city gets anywhere in the world.

As if mainland Spain didn't offer enough, who could forget Spain's two archipelagos? The Balearic Islands combine pretty beachside resorts, lively nightlife and celebrity glitz. Mallorca is the most-visited; Ibiza has trendy night spots; Menorca is family-oriented; and Formentera has great beaches.

Out in the Atlantic and nearer Africa than Spain are the volcanic Canary Islands. The largest, Tenerife, is home to Spain's highest peak, Mount Teide, and is refreshingly tropical in the north-west. Gran Canaria has been described as a continent in miniature, while barren Fuerteventura and Lanzarote have unbeatable beaches.

Whether you favour towering mountains or rolling plains, wild forests or city life, lively beach resorts or secluded bays, you'll find it all in Spain.

THE COAST OF SPAIN

From wide, sandy beaches to hidden, rocky coves, the extent and variety of Spain's coastline is mesmerizing.

T hink of the Spanish coast and you probably picture a sandy beach covered in neat rows of sun loungers, filled with holidaymakers basking in the hot southern sun. But there's so much more to the coast than that.

Firstly, the coastal scene shifts with each part of Spain you visit. At one extreme are the wild and beautiful crags of Galicia on the far north-western Atlantic coast, teeming with fish and as beautiful as they are dangerous for sailors. At the opposite extreme in every sense, is the Costa Cálida's Mar Menor, the warm, safe, sandy lagoon near the resort of La Manga in the south-east.

One thing that all sections of the coast have in common is that they are well looked after by the Spanish. With tourism such a major part of the economy, the

Above The pretty bay of Lafranc on the Costa Brava

authorities ensure that beaches are kept immaculate and meet European Blue Flag standards at all costs. The Blue Flags are awarded not just for cleanliness, but also for access and services, and Spain boasts 483 of them, 25 per cent more than their closest rival, Greece.

That same care goes into preserving the atmosphere of each beach. For those who prefer a crowded beach packed with bars and amusements, pedal-boats and waterskiing, there is no shortage, with every taste catered for in the big resorts. But for those who like a more natural ambience, stroll along any headland and you'll soon discover an isolated beach, even in popular places like Mallorca and the Costa del Sol. When it comes to property, you're less likely to find a bargain villa with a sea view these days, but you'll have no problem locating a reasonably priced seafront apartment at a fraction of what it would cost for a similar site on the coast of Britain.

THE COSTA BRAVA

The glorious beaches and countryside of Spain's 'Rugged Coast' have made it a popular destination since the 1970s. Today it's as beautiful as ever and enjoying a new lease of life.

The Costa Brava is one of the most picturesque coasts of Spain. Its pretty coves, fishing villages, historic castles and pine forests have long been a draw. Brits started travelling to the area in droves in the 1970s and as more hotels sprang up, it gained itself a reputation as a package-holiday destination. However, now many tour operators have removed Costa Brava resorts from their holiday brochures blaming 'destination fatigue.' But while the news that Lloret and Tossa de Mar are off the menu has been a serious blow to hotel and bar-owners there, it's the best possible news for those seeking an attractive, accessible second home. The Costa Brava remains the beautiful stretch of Spain it always was, it's just become more upmarket.

The Costa Brava, literally meaning the wild or rugged coast, stretches from Spain's French border in the north over 160 kilometres to Barcelona in the south. This coast is one of Spain's most attractive, with long stretches of golden sandy beaches interspersed with pine forests, dramatic crags and sheltered coves as the foothills of the Pyrenees meet the sea, all bathed in a classic Mediterranean climate of hot summers and mild winters.

The white port town of Cadaqués and the fishing town of Port de la Selva, in the far north, are just 20 kilometres from the French border and attract a discerning crowd of local Catalan holidaymakers and second-home owners from France. Round the headland is the Bay of Roses, and Roses itself, a fishing town that dates back to

Left The medieval village of Tossa de Mar is a delight to explore

Above A rooftop view across Barcelona with distinctive Gaudí-esque spires and curves

the eighth century when Greeks settled in the area. Unaffected by the mass tourist onslaught on nearby towns, Roses remains a quiet and relaxed resort, largely because its fishing industry and working culture have remained intact. It has several beaches that sweep round the bay and its natural beauty is enhanced by two nature reserves: the Cap de Creus peninsula, home to unique species of flora and fauna, and the Parc Natural dels Aiguamolls de l'Empordà, a reserve of flood plains, lakes, salt marshes and dunes, which are a haven for wildlife.

Heading south, next down is L'Estartit, a family resort on the coast situated at the foot of the Montgrí mountain range. L'Estartit boasts 15 kilometres of stunning rocky coastline and one of the longest sandy beaches on the Costa Brava. Once a quiet fishing village, it retains the quaint charm of a harbour,

but also has a modern yacht marina from which glass-bottomed boat trips depart for the Medes Islands, an archipelago of seven islands that are an important marine reserve and a top destination for scuba divers.

Inland, away from the coast, the two major towns of Figueres and medieval Girona are great assets to the region. Figueres is the birthplace of the Costa Brava's favourite son, the surrealist artist Salvador Dalí, and home to the Teatre-Museu Dalí, a five-floor house dedicated to his extraordinary paintings and sculptures. The walled city of Girona was originally a Roman settlement and has been

A KNIGHT'S DOMAIN

"It was the view that did it!" says Bea, when she explains why she and her husband Steve fell in love with the "total ruin" they found on top of a hill.

The couple have restored a thirteenth-century country house near medieval Girona to create their dream home.

It sits in five acres of open country, but is just half an hour from Girona airport, with the spectacular coastal scenery of the Costa Brava a short drive away.

Originally from Surrey, the couple wanted a change in lifestyle. They bought the tumbledown chapel and priory for €240,000 in 2002 and have spent two years restoring it with the help of local artisans.

It's been hard work – the property was without electricity or water, and, says Steve: "Old buildings have a life of their own."

Today, the couple rent out their six-bed house during the summer, and they've built their own living accommodation in a barn close by.

much fought over through the ages. Today, it is known for its medieval architecture, especially in the former Jewish quarter, and has been dubbed the 'New Barcelona' for its trendy restaurants, smart shops and cool, moneyed, ambience.

Head south-east from Girona for Tossa de Mar on the coast and the more boisterous southern Costa Brava begins. Tossa is an attractive town with cobbled streets and a busy beach. Its claim to fame dates back to the 1950s, when Ava Gardner and Frank Sinatra made a film around the town; a statue of the leading lady was erected in her honour.

Lloret de Mar is the liveliest resort on the coast, with dozens of British-style bars and clubs. It's a town whose appeal is largely for the under-30s, but it does have its charms for the young family, with five safe and sandy beaches and Europe's biggest water park, Waterworld. Lloret has its fair share of culture, too, with grand public buildings that remain from its glory days as a prosperous

port in the eighteenth and nineteenth centuries. A further five kilometres down the coast is Blanes, a quieter family resort, but one that attracts an international crowd.

Just an hour's drive further south is Barcelona, the Catalan capital with everything you could ask for in a great city: chic café culture, a beach, a port, gorgeous shops, the world-famous Ramblas, and architectural splendours such as the Sagrada Familia created by Gaudí.

So what kind of houses are on offer, and at what price? The attractions of the Costa Brava inevitably make it a more expensive prospect for house-buyers, especially as it is easily reachable for weekenders from northern Europe. It's unlikely that you'll find the renovation bargains that you might in remoter areas, but as the package tourists have moved on so a new stock of villas has come on the market. A basic two-bedroom villa in L'Estartit is likely to cost in the region of £150,000, while a more luxurious home with pool and sea views would leave little change from £300,000. Inland, property is less expensive but not dramatically so, especially in the foothills of the Pyrenees with its closeness to the ski resorts.

IN BRIEF

Nearest airports: Girona and Barcelona

Main city: Girona

Language: Catalan and Castilian Spanish

Climate: Warm summers and mild springs but winters can be chilly: 11°C January; 24°C August.

Most famous son: Salvador Dalí. Born in Figueres in 1904, he lived over half his adult life at Port Lligat. The Costa Brava is dotted with reminders of Dalí, not least his museum at Figueres and homes at Port Lligat and Púbol.

Not to be missed: Exploring the coves and limpid waters along the coastline; visiting medieval stone villages such as Pals and Besalú; a stroll around Cadaqués, the area's prettiest whitewashed village and a Dalí favourite; a snorkelling trip to the Illes Medes, the Costa Brava's underwater nature reserve.

COSTA DORADA

Costa Dorada means 'Golden Coast', but broad sandy beaches shimmering in the sunshine are only half the story; this region has far more to offer.

The Costa Dorada is one of the lesser known Spanish coasts. It starts where the Costa Brava finishes south of Barcelona, and runs for 300 kilometres along Catalonia's south coast, north of the Valencia region. It offers easy accessibility from the UK to Reus airport via budget airlines and borders rural Catalonia.

It's one of the last places on Spain's eastern or southern coasts where you can still snap up a bargain property. Beach-front homes inevitably attract a premium, but go just beyond the front-line and you could well find a pretty village house with a terrace overlooking vineyards on one side and with a glimpse of the sea on the other. There's also the opportunity to make a living from rural tourism, as hiking and outdoor activities in the region are up-and-coming. Offering farmhouse accommodation is an excellent option, especially as the local government offers grants to help breathe life into over-tranquil communities.

Although not as developed or as attractive in some ways as the Costa Brava, the Costa Dorada's beaches are popular with Spanish and foreign families each summer, especially in Salou and Sitges. Salou is more family oriented, with the Port Aventura theme park nearby, while Sitges is a party town: hipper and with a terrific gay scene, especially at its world-renowned carnival each February. But the Costa Dorada has history and culture too. The capital of the region is Tarragona, now a lively, modern, industrial city but once known as Imperial Tarraco, the most important city in the Roman Empire after

Left The beach at L'Ametlla de Mar is typical of much of the coastline

Above The fortified walls of Tarragona

"With such a varied and attractive coastline, you could be forgiven for ignoring the interior of the province, yet it offers amazingly varied and spectacular scenery"

Rome itself. Remains include the amphitheatre by the sea and the magnificent Roman aqueduct that towers over the landscape. There are several UNESCO World Heritage Sites to visit, as well as the birthplaces of geniuses like Antoni Gaudí and Pau Casals.

At the southern end of the coast lies the Ebro River Delta, one of the Med's most important marine reserves, while at the northern end is the beautiful Garraf National Park. Between these, the Costa Dorada is a large, unspoiled, peaceful province where you can play golf in mild sunshine all year round amidst olive and almond groves, or cycle, walk or horse-ride through quiet green hills. You can go bird-watching in one of Spain's most

Left Rice paddies in the fertile Ebro Delta – in contrast to the mountains to the north, and vines and almond groves of the coastal plain, the delta is flat and filled with dunes and lakes

important ecological reserves, or watch one of the Mediterranean's last working fishing fleets come into port. By night, you can eat the fresh catch at a local restaurant overlooking the harbour, or take a boat out on the Ebro, Spain's greatest river.

The Ebro Delta is the second most important wetland in the Mediterranean and heaven for birdwatchers. In contrast to the mountains in the north and the vines and almond and hazel groves of the coastal plain, the delta is flat, blue and soothing, filled with white dunes, lakes and exotic vegetation.

With such an attractive coast, you could be forgiven for ignoring the interior of the province. And yet it is amazingly fascinating and varied. To the west of the Ebro rises one of Spain's most interesting mountainous areas, the Gredos Mountains, standing between Catalonia, Valencia and Aragón. Nature lovers will be entranced by the wild landscapes, forests and rich fauna, including wild goats and foraging boars.

When it comes to property, the Costa Dorada divides neatly into coast and inland. On the coast, Sitges is the most northern resort and also one of the liveliest places to

SUNSHINE HOLIDAYS

Tim and Vivienne Williams bought a four-bed farmhouse near Vilafranca, just inland from the Costa Dorada, for £66,000 and have spent another £80,000 on renovations. "We wanted to be in the countryside somewhere quiet, and liked Catalonia because it's less hot and more seasonal than the south," says Tim.

They found the buying process smooth, using a local estate agent but an English-born surveyor. The one hiccup in the purchase was having to buy more land than they originally wanted, as agricultural land can't be split up into parcels. But now they're pleased to have a larger garden than they'd planned.

The house needed a new roof and the interior had to be completely gutted, all of which was completed by a Spanish builder who'd been recommended by the estate agent.

The couple use the house for holidays and are looking forward to retiring there one day. But as they're only in their late thirties, they've a while to wait for that pleasure!

live on this costa. Its proximity to Barcelona means it is popular with city dwellers looking for weekend fun, and prices are high.

Further down the coast, Salou and Cambrils offer lots of apartments and villas but again, at a price. Houses in the old town of Cambrils, with its quiet narrow streets and flower-filled balconies, are highly coveted and very expensive too. Further down the coast, L'Hospitalet, L'Ampolla and L'Ametlla de Mar are unspoiled and not so pricey.

The real gems of the Costa Dorada are to be found inland, in the Priorat wine country or the hills of the Conca de Barberà, and in particular around the Ebro Valley. Closer to Reus airport and the sea, and just an hour's drive from Barcelona, the Alt Camp is a peaceful grape and hazelnut-growing area. Farmhouses and village houses can still be found here for a reasonable price, and although the flat landscape may lack the views of the Ebro Valley, it is popular with cyclists so rural tourism is on the rise.

For those seeking a challenge, renovating ruined farmhouses can be profitable as well as useful for the region. Smallholdings of little use to the local agricultural economy are being refurbished and enjoyed once again, bringing life and building jobs to old communities. Look around the Ebro Valley, or near little towns like Falset or Tivissa, or the mountains of the Conca de Barberà.

"The British are into places that even the Catalans don't know about," explains one property agent. "You can buy a large chunk of land that comes with olive groves, a shack, and incredible views in the Tortosa area for £35,000," says another agent, Rita Fryer of www.thepropertyfinders.com. But beware: restoration will cost another £35,000.

The Costa Dorada boom has already started, but even as prices increase, there are still bargains to be found.

IN BRIEF

Nearest airports: Reus and Barcelona

Main city: Tarragona

Language: Catalan and Castilian Spanish

Climate: Mild and temperate Mediterranean climate with 7 to 10°C in winter and 20 to 25°C in summer. It's a couple of degrees cooler inland.

Most famous son: Gaudí. An architect born in Reus in 1852, his modernistic designs in Barcelona were a totally Spanish take on Art Nouveau and set the template for the trend-setting city Barcelona is today. There are 24 modernist buildings in Reus, too.

Not to be missed: View the Roman remains in Tarragona and the vast Ebro wetlands. For some action, head to the Port Aventura theme park with its exotic attractions. Don't miss the traditional Catalan staples – the Sardana dance and the human castles – at any of the many annual festivals.

COSTA BLANCA

Spain's 'White Coast' boasts perfect white sands and almost permanently blue skies. No wonder it remains a perennial favourite for Brits.

The Costa Blanca holds a special place in British hearts, with many choosing to retire to the 'White Coast' or buy a holiday home there. The main towns are Benidorm, Dénia and Moraira in the north, and Torrevieja and Guardamar in the south. Neatly bisecting the two sides is Alicante, the region's business centre and home to the international airport. Other airport options are at Valencia in the north and Murcia's San Javier airport to the south.

The Costa Blanca officially begins at Gandía, at the end of the fast Renfe railway line. Though as many as 3,000 of its 60,000 citizens are British, Gandía retains a true Spanish holiday atmosphere as each summertime its apartment blocks fill with Spaniards seeking relief from the searing heat of the interior.

Heading south, along the twisting mountain road that hugs the coast, or the fast new toll motorway that runs alongside it, the next major town is Dénia; originally a Greek settlement and named after the goddess

Above Looking out to sea from Dénia

Above right The rocky coastline near Jávea

"Gandía retains a holiday atmosphere as each summer its apartment blocks fill wih Spaniards seeking relief from the heat of the interior"

Diana. As well as boasting a magnificent castle, Dénia is home to an impressive marina, a tree-lined promenade and long sandy beaches.

Nearby, on the other side of the imposing Mount Montgó, is Jávea. This town has been built around an unusual fortified church that forms one of its three distinct characteristics – the others being the beach and port. Jávea has a north-European feel, with almost a third of the town's resident population being of non-Spanish origin.

As the coast swings out to form the high headland, there are several inland areas – such as the Jalón Valley – with picturesque villages that are just a few minutes' drive from the coast, but a world away in terms of property prices. Here you'll find many of the benefits of the coast, along

with non-touristy village charm and friendly cafés serving a three course *'menú del día'* for just €8 including bread, salad, olives and wine! But for those who simply must be by the seaside, round the headland is the charming town of Moraira. It has a marina and several good sandy beaches, including the gently shelving Playa L'Ampolla beach, which is ideal for children. From here, you can gaze at Ibiza just a few miles across the Med, or the impressive Peñón de Ifach headland at Calpe.

Most villas in the area are built *pueblo*-style and strict local planning restrictions have kept high-rise developments out of the towns, ensuring they retain their traditional character. This is especially true in Calpe, which has avoided high-rise hotel development along its two sandy beaches (which are joined by a pretty shoreline promenade over a mile long). Ernest Hemingway spent his summers here in the 1930s, but the crowds that descend each summer ensure he would barely recognise it today. Calpe is

Left A typical Costa Blanca villa to be found on one of the many *urbanizaciones* (developments)

especially popular with the Germans and Belgians who, added to the Brits, form a greater part of the population than the Spanish. The last stop before reaching Benidorm is Altea, regarded by many as the jewel in the Costa Blanca's crown. The old town is a picturesque maze of white houses and narrow streets, with terrific shops and a vibrant social scene.

And so to Benidorm, a forest of high-rise apartment blocks and hotels. Much maligned over the years for mass tourism and kiss-me-quick standards, the resort has matured and is now known for its pleasant family atmosphere. It is also home to huge sandy beaches that win Blue Flags every year, along with enough theme parks to keep kids happy through the longest holiday. The area is a golfing paradise, too, with 14 courses and a climate that allows play all year round.

Lying at the centre of the Costa Blanca is Alicante, the coast's capital. Ironically it's the place that most visitors to the region never see – annually some six million land at the airport and speedily head for the resorts north and south. They are missing plenty. The city has undergone a regeneration over the past two decades that has seen the previously

A LITTLE MORE SUN!

Mick and Lin Cope own a mountain-top villa inland of the Costa Blanca, near Alicante, and are now able to divide their time between England and Spain. "We just wanted to let a little more sun into our life," explains Mick, "and we've achieved that thanks to the wonderful low-cost airlines! It's easier to commute from Essex to Alicante than it is to get to Manchester."

They've now achieved a balanced life, where Mick can work as an author in the cool room overlooking the pool, while Lin enjoys the sun and potters around in her ever-greener garden. Mick also loves riding his Harley-Davidson motorbike along the quiet Spanish roads, while Lin has taken up painting.

They're both happy that they're able to still live like teenagers, unlike their parents' generation, for whom hitting 50 was a signal to slow down. "For us, life has never been richer," they say.

> *"The Sierra de la Serrella is a land of historic towns and sleepy villages, with eagles flying above an unspoiled landscape of wild flowers, almonds, olives and herbs"*

down-at-heel centre become a setting for a bustling café and restaurant scene, with excellent shops and a castle that was held by the British in the seventeenth century until Spanish forces retook it by blowing it up.

The British find a warmer welcome these days in the town of Torrevieja. To some it's overdeveloped and a bit boisterous, but others love its bustling promenade. There are good beaches in the immediate vicinity and golfers are spoiled for choice with 3 championship golf courses within 20 kilometres, at Villamartín, Las Ramblas and Royal Campoamor.

Property prices around the Costa Blanca vary enormously. A terraced two-bed townhouse in Oliva can cost £50,000, while a smart four-bed villa with pool in Dénia will cost some £250,000. Inland, again, prices drop sharply, even though the countryside is beautiful. In the north, the Sierra de

Above From the Costa Blanca at Dénia, you can gaze out to sea to the Balearic island of Ibiza – in fact, should you fancy a change of scene, you can very easily take a ferry there

la Serrella, a short drive from Benidorm, is a land of historic towns and sleepy villages, with eagles flying above an unspoiled landscape of wild flowers, olives and herbs.

Elche, a few miles inland from Alicante, is the region's second most important town. It is famous for its 300,000 date palms, lively annual carnival and shoe- and sandal-making. Further south, the historic town of Orihuela livens up a somewhat featureless plain inland from Torrevieja. Here, vast salt pans and marshes resist development and bargains are to be had by the house-hunter who is willing to go that extra mile.

IN BRIEF

Nearest airports: Alicante and San Javier at Murcia

Main city: Alicante

Language: Valencian (a dialect of Catalan) and Castilian Spanish

Climate: Pleasant, though summer temperatures reach 40ºC and even in winter it rarely goes below 10ºC. Daytime in winter often reaches 20ºC. Little rain falls until autumn, when it is frequently torrential.

Not to be missed: The sumptuous Parisian-style cabaret at the Benidorm Palace isn't something you see every day. Neither is the spectacular Palm Forest of Elche, Europe's largest, through which you can take a ride on a tourist train. But what you really have to do is explore the pretty seaside towns, such as Moraira, Altea and Calpe, splash about in the sea, make sandcastles and enjoy being a big kid.

COSTA CÁLIDA

The Costa Cálida, or 'Warm Coast', is a stretch of the Spanish coastline that has escaped the large-scale development found in the more well-known costas.

This area, which stretches between the Mar Menor in the north and the picturesque town of Águilas in the south, has long been a favourite amongst the Spanish.

Over the decades, the authorities in Murcia enviously watched their neighbours on the nearby Costa Blanca and Costa del Sol profiting from the growth of the north-European market, until they resolved to get a slice of the action for themselves. They radically improved the tourist infrastructure and awarded themselves the new name of Costa Cálida. Now, improved road links and a new runway at Murcia airport (a whole new international airport is coming to nearby Corvera in 2007) make this coast a fantastic prospect as a place to buy and live.

Why the attraction? Well, the weather for starters. The World Health Organisation cites the Costa Cálida as having one of the healthiest climates in the world with an average of 320 days of sunshine each year and a sea temperature that rarely dips below 17°C. The weather is terrific for at least 10 months of the year, allowing year-round golf on the dozen or so new courses. The surrounding land, though semi-desert, is also a haven for wildlife including rare eagles and tortoises.

Then there are the beaches, starting in the north at the Mar Menor (literally the 'Smaller Sea'), which is Europe's largest saltwater lagoon. It's a haven for water sports enthusiasts as the water temperature is several degrees warmer than elsewhere on the coast and it's almost entirely closed off from the Mediterranean by the La Manga strip and another headland. The area is popular with Spanish holidaymakers, and its

AMANDA SAYS

"DON'T FORGET THAT THE BEST BARGAINS HERE ARE OFTEN TO BE FOUND INLAND WHERE THE LANDSCAPE IS DOMINATED BY VINEYARDS, RIVERS, MOUNTAINS AND APRICOT TREES."

Left Fishing boats are a familiar sight on the Costa Cálida

"Improved road links and the new international airport coming to nearby Corvera (due to open in 2007) make this coast a fantastic prospect"

relaxed atmosphere tends to appeal to families rather than a younger crowd. In particular, many older people come for the health-giving properties attributed to the Mar Menor, with its high iodine and salt concentration. Don't be surprised to see people sitting beside the sea encrusted in mud.

Travelling south along the coastline and around the Mar Menor, you pass through a number of small resorts before reaching slightly inland Santiago de la Ribera and Los Alcázares, an old health spa. The scenery here is a cross between farmland and seascapes defined by windmills, palm and lemon trees, and the resorts of Los Urrutias, Los Nietos and Cabo de Palos. Then you reach the La Manga strip, literally 'the sleeve' of the mainland. Here, sprinklers water perfect lawns in a 1,500-acre, security-guarded enclave of

well-off Brits. It's not everyone's cup of tea, but for those who like their Spain not too Spanish, La Manga has plenty to offer, including superb golf and tennis facilities, and a private beach. Stay before a major football championship and be warned, you might have to rough it with the Beckhams!

Heading back in a loop from the strip, the coastal road passes through a rocky, mountainous region peppered with abandoned mines in the valleys and wind farms on the hills, before reaching La Unión, once famous for its silver mines. The next stop, just five miles away, is the province's second city and major port, Cartagena. One of Spain and Europe's most important ports for more than 2,000 years, Cartagena is an impressive city, much of whose history remains visible. Heavily fortified to repel would-be invaders, the sea ramparts are of Roman origin and today flank the esplanade, along whose upper deck locals and visitors alike stroll to take in the sea views before heading into the historic city centre and smart shops.

Leaving Cartagena and driving south along the coast, the scenery becomes increasingly dramatic before reaching the Gulf of Mazarrón. Here, the swathes of

A WARM WELCOME

No one could accuse Brendan and Moira O'Reilly from Dublin of rushing into their move to Spain. They bought off-plan a 'quad' (one house of a group of four) in Los Alcázares in October 2002, and were finally ready to make the move full-time in October 2005, having seen the area develop into a charming and friendly community.

Apart from the wonderful climate and good friends to enjoy it with, Brendan and Moira like exploring the picturesque local towns like Lorca, Cartagena and Murcia.

With the difference in price between their old home in Dublin and their new one in Spain, they were able to buy a flat in Dublin which they rent out to their daughter, with a guaranteed room for them when they want to visit.

To help make friends in the town, Brendan has taken a TEFL qualification, and is switching football allegiances to his local Spanish team!

"The World Health Organisation cites the Costa Cálida as having one of the healthiest climates in the world with an average of 320 days of sunshine each year"

golden beaches are interspersed with rocky coves, some secluded and empty, others with just a bar. They make a contrast to the flat, shallow coast to the north. Lastly, having driven through oleander-covered slopes, you reach the fishing town of Águilas, home to some beautiful buildings, a fifteenth-century castle, pleasant beaches and one of the wildest Mardi Gras carnivals in Spain.

Head inland through the beautiful Sierra de Carrascoy and you come to Murcia, the region's capital city. Set on the left bank of the River Segura, Murcia is a university town with more culture and excitement than you might expect in this hot corner of Spain.

Away from the Mar Menor, the Costa Cálida is being developed in a sympathetic but purposeful way. Rather than higgledy-piggledy clusters of villas dotting the landscape, large golf villages of several thousand homes are being built. These have all the benefits of security, instant social connections, well-managed golf courses and attractive – if a tad artificial – water features.

For the retired or families with young children, the Costa Cálida's ambience, good infrastructure and affordable prices are strong lures, with two-bed apartments near to the beach and golf courses from £90,000. A three-bed villa with private pool would set you back around £270,000 in Mar Menor, but more inside the gates of La Manga.

Rural property prices have sky-rocketed in the past year, but you can still buy an attractive farmhouse with breathtaking mountain views and several acres of olive and almond trees for under £150,000, even with the coast less than a half hour's drive away.

Prospective purchasers should know, though, that a pleasant climate on the coast can feel like a raging furnace inland without cool sea breezes. Also, be sure to visit at various times of the year because fields carpeted in wild flowers in April may be barren and parched for the rest of the year.

IN BRIEF

Nearest airports: San Javier at Murcia, Alicante and Valencia. (A new Murcia international airport is due to open at Corvera in 2007)

Main city: Murcia

Language: Castilian Spanish

Climate: Hot, but not too hot. While daytime temperatures rarely fall below 30ºC in summer, they also rarely fall below 18ºC in winter. Rain is very scarce with an average of over 320 sunny days each year.

Not to be missed: A dip in the Mar Menor: this is a natural lagoon that is more salty than the Mediterranean – the locals believe it has health-giving properties. A trip inland to the beautiful Ricote Valley where the River Segura irrigates a fertile landscape of palm trees, olive and orange groves. For shopping, take yourself to Murcia or Cartagena, both beautiful, historic cities.

COSTA DE ALMERÍA

Almería offers great inland scenery and a superb coastal environment. Huge investment in the infrastructure has opened the region to buyers after great weather and lower prices.

I n a land of property hot spots, the Costa de Almería is the hottest of all. This often harsh and arid land is the closest thing that Europe has to a desert, and its sandy landscape has been used as a backdrop for all sorts of films from *Lawrence of Arabia* to *The Good, the Bad and the Ugly*. But as the desert has been tamed and brought to bloom by huge investment and irrigation, orange and lemon plantations have turned the land green and the property developers have moved in, creating holiday-home *pueblos* as well as more environmentally-sensitive developments.

Until recently, the geography and poor transport infrastructure of this costa kept it relatively unspoiled and untouched. It's been described as a poor relation to both the Costa del Sol in the south and Costa Blanca in the north, but many people value it for that undeveloped charm. The property market heated up in 2004 when easyJet announced the beginning of services to Almería airport, which meant visitors no longer had to do the longer drive down from Murcia airport or up from Málaga. Another vital change was Almería's staging of the Mediterranean Games in 2005 and the huge investment in infrastructure that this brought about, with new motorways and spending on prettifying the towns and resorts.

For all these reasons, plus high prices elsewhere, homes have increased in price by at least a quarter over the past year, but are still relatively cheap compared to their northern and southern equivalents. Foreign buyers are

Left The attractive whitewashed town of Mojácar

Above A gated community near Almerimar

"Prices on the Costa de Almería are still relatively good compared to the Costa del Sol and Costa Blanca"

being attracted by both the sandy beaches and the rugged beauty inland. That beauty begins in the south with the ancient city of Adra, 'gateway to the Alpujarras' and one of Spain's most ancient settlements. Next is Roquetas de Mar, a popular resort with beautiful beaches, a pretty harbour and cosmopolitan restaurants and bars. Sports facilities are excellent here, with all the usual watersports plus golf and pony trekking inland.

A little further along the coast is the resort of Almerimar, one of the driest places in Europe. Similar to Roquetas, Almerimar has great beaches and sports facilities, and is also just a short drive from southern Spain's premier ski resort in the Sierra Nevada mountains. Heading back along the coast past Almería city is the resort of Carboneras, a town largely built in a traditional Moorish style. Carboneras was home to film director David Lean for many years after he fell in love with the village while filming *Lawrence of Arabia* in the 1960s.

Ten miles along is the Costa de Almería's best-known town, Mojácar, which has two distinct parts – an old town and modern beach resort. The old town, Mojácar Pueblo, sits on top of a steep-sided hill two kilometres inland, overlooking the Mediterranean. Often likened to a pile of sugar cubes thanks to its whitewashed houses, the town's charm lies in its picturesque streets and balconies that overflow with bougainvillea. During the 1960s it was a popular hangout for artists and, despite its obvious tourist appeal, in the off-season Mojácar Pueblo remains a pretty and unassuming town with a laid-back atmosphere. The resort, Mojácar Playa, is the

AMANDA SAYS

"THE ALMERÍA PROVINCE HAS BENEFITED FROM THE RECENT 15TH MEDITERRANEAN GAMES, WHICH SAW A BIG INJECTION OF INVESTMENT INTO THE AREA'S FACILITIES AND INFRASTRUCTURE."

Above Almería has seafront properties at affordable prices

result of government investment in the 1970s, when the coast was opened up to the outside world, bringing jobs and prosperity. It offers a long beach with a string of hotels and restaurants.

Vera Playa lies just outside Mojácar and is most famous for its eight kilometres of sandy beaches. There is also an entire urbanisation for naturists, where you can swim, sunbathe, shop and eat out 365 days a year dressed in just suntan lotion and a smile.

The Costa de Almería ends in the north with San Juan de Los Terreros, a small resort still undergoing development that will soon be home to new golf courses. Moving inland, the buzz in recent months has been about the Almanzora Valley and its main town, Albox. As much as 15 per cent of its

INLAND ALMERÍA

"I just knew this was the house for me, and I knew Mick felt the same when he squeezed my hand and smiled." So says Gail Harris of her 200-year-old farmhouse, Cortijo del Sevillano, near Cuevas de Almanzora, where she and partner Mick Thorburn run a B&B.

They chose Almería because they knew they could purchase a stunning country home for a price that would only buy a standard villa on the Costa del Sol. But it wouldn't have been possible without the improvements in transport links of recent years that enable Mick to continue his business as an advertising broker back home. He makes frequent trips to London but does the rest of his work by phone and Internet.

The couple now spend one week of each month in London so Mick can get in 'face-time' with clients. They value the long summers and short winters, and have a relaxing lifestyle of daytimes at the beach and evenings eating in local restaurants or entertaining guests.

Above The Moorish castle, or Alcazaba, provides a stunning backdrop to Almería city port

population is now made up of British expats and the town has recently seen the opening of its first Chinese takeaway.

As usual in Spain, you don't have to travel far inland to find plots of land that escape the interest of major property developers. Out in the sierras and plains are any number of abandoned *cortijos* and *fincas* waiting to be returned to full glory. The prospective buyer can find out who owns these through the local land registry and then simply make an

offer. Another option for inland buyers is cave houses. Carved out of the soft sandstone around Cuevas de Almanzora and Baza, they are reminiscent of North African troglodyte communities but far more sophisticated.

On the coast, new developments in the areas of Vera and Garrucha will be affordable and benefit from a warmer off-season climate than anywhere else in mainland Spain. A two-bedroom apartment with communal pool close to the beach will cost around £130,000, while a four-bedroom villa with pool will go from £200,000.

COSTA DEL SOL

Still famous after all these years, the Costa del Sol has an enduring appeal and remains the California of Europe thanks to its climate, way of life and work opportunities.

W here in the world can you ski in the morning and sunbathe on your yacht in the afternoon? California or Lake Geneva, maybe. But where can you enjoy a 'full English' for breakfast, stroll round a Moorish palace before lunch and relax with tapas and dry *fino* in a picturesque white village in the evening? Just one place – the Costa del Sol.

For many Britons, their love affair with Spain began here with package holidays in the 1960s and 1970s. Back then, Marbella was a fishing village and beachfront plots were as cheap as chips. Now Marbella is bling-city, favoured by Europe's beautiful people, and beachfront plots are for the super-rich. Stunning apartment complexes sit on once remote promontories and one-time donkey pastures are golf courses, with 40 in the area at the last count and as many again being planned.

Those changes have brought some problems – when people refer to places as being 'unspoiled', they're probably not talking about this stretch of coast – but even so, disparaging references to the Costa del Concrete are well off the mark. The attractions that first drew us in droves remain: sun, sea, sand and a more relaxed way of life. The area is blessed with temperatures that rarely sink below 16°C in winter (except in the hills) and settle at around 35°C in the summer. There's a healthy outdoor lifestyle that revolves around water sports, golf, superb shopping and restaurants,

"*The attractions that first drew us in droves to the Costa del Sol still remain: sun, sea and sand, and a more relaxed way of life*"

wonderful walking country, and – an important factor for many – a British population who live and work in the area. Budget flights from every part of the UK mean that 'euro-commuting' is a serious option.

The Costa del Sol runs for around 160 kilometres from Gibraltar to Motril. If there is a part of the costa still under-developed, it's the first 25 kilometres that leads to Estepona, a charming coastal resort that has retained its Spanish character. The old town's cobbled streets are home to dozens of cafés and tapas bars serving traditional Spanish delicacies, and Estepona marina, at the western end of the promenade, is the perfect spot for a twilight stroll.

Above Upmarket yachts in the harbour of Puerto Banús

Next along the coast is Puerto Banús, an upmarket marina where luxury yachts are moored alongside swanky boutiques and bars. Here you can rub shoulders with the likes of celebrity publicist Max Clifford or Simon '*Pop Idol*' Cowell. The marina features a casino, Corte Inglés department store, marine observatory and a multiplex cinema.

Lovely as Puerto Banús is, if the Costa del Sol were a Monopoly board, it is Marbella's Golden Mile a little further down the coast that would be Mayfair. Prices for desirable properties have sky-rocketed since new Russian and Middle-Eastern money arrived. The late King Fahd of Saudi Arabia even built a full-size replica of the White House here.

Marbella is also a popular spot for well-heeled Spaniards such as Antonio Banderas and Julio Iglesias. The town hasn't always been so affluent, however, but it was rescued from tawdriness in the 1980s, thanks largely to the colourful Jesús Gil, one-time mayor and businessman. It was only after

his recent death that it transpired Gil had been selling planning permissions on the side. This revelation caused consternation in the property market that is still being smoothed out today. It has also forced the Regional Government of Andalusia to look at ways of preserving this part of Spain.

Still heading east towards the region's capital, Málaga, Mijas is a typical Andalusian village, with spectacular views of the coast. Indeed the hinterland of the costa is strewn with these 'white villages' – so called because of their sugar-cube, Moorish-style white-washed houses – from Casares in the west to the villages of the Alpujarras in the east. Long after northern Europeans came holidaying on the coast, these villages remained utterly Spanish, their alleyways and picturesque squares echoing to the clip-clop of passing donkeys. It is still possible to buy a little town house here and feel part of a truly Spanish community.

At the other end of the scale is Torremolinos, the original package-holiday destination. Such places, with often woefully outdated notoriety, provide excellent opportunities for snapping up bargains.

Málaga, often overlooked in the rush to

DOING IT THEMSELVES

When Peter and Carol Smith arrived in Lake Viñuela, near Málaga, from Hampshire five years ago, they had pleasant notions of watching a team of builders putting together their dream home.

But when they started work, they found they enjoyed it so much they just kept on going and did it all themselves! They built such a big and beautiful home that they've decided to offer some rooms for B&B. Says Carol: "We're now open for business and enjoying life to the full on our mountaintop."

Carol and Peter's Spanish is coming along too, improving from the 'builder's' Spanish they picked up when building their home: "Locals call in for water for their mules or to fill up the backpacks they use to spray the vines and they love to stop and chat about any local news," says Peter.

They've also got to know a group of expats and evenings of drinks around the barbecue have become a regular occurrence.

get to the resorts, has an attractive downtown packed with plazas, cafés and art galleries, as befits the birthplace of Picasso. There are also reminders of the port's Roman and Moorish past, such as the fortified Alcazaba Palace which overlooks the city.

Fifty kilometres from Málaga at Nerja, the Costa del Sol becomes the Costa Tropical. Once a quiet fishing village, the town now has a population of 12,000 and is popular with second-home owners from the UK, drawn here by the 16 kilometres of sandy beaches. Marina developments around Almuñécar extend the coastline outwards, a neat solution that keeps the countryside villa-free. Continuing eastwards, the climate does become more tropical, with Salobreña poking out from plantations of avocado, mango and custard apple. The costa finally ends at Motril, in the shadow of the Sierra Nevada mountain range which stretches 3,500 metres into the clear blue sky and offers quality skiing from December until May.

The traditional notion of the Brit homeowner in southern Spain – probably an ex-footballer now dedicating his life to golf – is starting to change. While golf is indeed huge business and the warm climate favours the retired, a younger, hipper type of purchaser is buying property slightly inland, prompted particularly by Chris Stewart's book *Driving over Lemons*. Now, yoga centres and artistic retreats are breathing new life into villages that had seen so many of their youngsters move out in search of work.

As more Brits move here, so too do the professionals to serve them, whether it's British doctors and lawyers or swimming pool repairers and plumbers. They are bringing their families, too, prompting the development of good international schools.

Can this growth continue? With 250,000 homes being built in 2005, it appears that you should still be able to buy an affordable home in the region. The only change is that the massive house price rises of some 25 per cent per annum in recent years have slowed down, so these homes don't present a brilliant investment opportunity. But having said that, there are few better places to enjoy life than on the Costa del Sol.

IN BRIEF

Nearest airports: Málaga, Granada, Gibraltar

Main city: Málaga

Language: Castilian Spanish

Climate: Hot in summer, with temperatures often above 40ºC – the *siesta* was invented here. Winters are mild on the coast, often up to 22ºC in the daytime, but can be chilly in the mountains.

Most famous son: Pablo Picasso, born in 1881 in Málaga, but it wasn't until 30 years after his death in 1973 that Málaga opened a museum worthy of him, the Museo Picasso Málaga, containing 204 works of art reckoned to be worth around £122 million.

Not to be missed: For culture, the Picasso museum; for history, Granada and its twelfth-century Moorish palace the Alhambra; and for fun, the seaside.

COSTA DE LA LUZ

In some ways it's the final frontier. Home to miles of Atlantic beaches, a vast national park and historic inland towns, this coast is one of Spain's most wild and unspoiled.

T he wildly beautiful Costa de la Luz stretches from the Portuguese border in the west almost to Gibraltar in the east. While the neighbouring Algarve and Costa del Sol were being relentlessly developed, this costa lay back and enjoyed the Atlantic breezes. But now, all kinds of inherent advantages have put the Costa de la Luz on the map for British property buyers, not least the vast strips of white sand, backed by dunes and pine forests.

Just a little inland is the Sherry Triangle based around Jerez de la Frontera, while nearby Doñana National Park is one of the largest wildlife reserves in Europe and home to Europe's only big cat, the lynx. Then there's the romantic shabby-chic of Cádiz. All of this amidst 300 days of sunshine a year and cooling Atlantic breezes that take the edge off the heat. It's little wonder that the Spanish choose this costa as their holiday destination of choice. And with four international airports serving the region – Jerez, Gibraltar, Seville and Faro, just half an hour away over the border – we Brits are following the Spanish lead.

The 'Coast of Light', as it literally translates, can be split into two parts, with the Doñana National Park dividing them. The eastern half starts at Tarifa, where Europe and Africa almost touch. Although it has been a trading port since prehistoric times, in Tarifa these days, life is all about the beach. The shore is dotted with windsurfers while above brightly coloured surf-kites flutter in the blue sky. As Europe's unofficial windsurfing capital, it attracts a younger, cooler crowd along with those who prefer a more low-key type of nightlife to the glitz of the Costa del Sol. The town's compact, maze-like centre – reminiscent of Marrakech – is home to traditional riads (houses built around a central courtyard) as well as contemporary apartments.

Left The attractive port town of Ayamonte

"All kinds of advantages have put the Costa de la Luz on the map, not least the vast strips of white sand, backed by dunes and pine forests"

Beyond Tarifa, this part of the costa sweeps on with 90 kilometres of glorious beaches. Strict building restrictions have helped to safeguard their raw beauty from the worst ravages of mass tourism. Typical is Bolonia beach, a horseshoe-shaped lip of sandy shoreline, accessible only via a single-track road leading down to the seashore through the hills. A ruined Roman fort overlooks the sands, but otherwise it's possible to have the whole beach to yourself. For many newcomers to the Costa de la Luz, it is this tranquillity and unspoiled scenery that most appeals.

Fishing is a big feature of the province, and nowhere more so than the charming Zahara de los Atunes, a whitewashed village which Spanish holidaymakers have kept to themselves for long enough! Back on the main road, the impressive citadel town of Vejer de la Frontera is built on top of a mountain and has been voted the prettiest hilltop town in Spain. It has also been named a heritage site by the Spanish Government. The last town before

Cádiz is Chiclana, popular with Brits due to its central position and minutes from the upmarket beaches of La Barrosa.

Cádiz is virtually encircled by the sea and as the last stop between Spain and the New World, it became rich on gold looted by conquistadors. Most of its impressive buildings, such as the golden domed cathedral that dominates the seafront promenade, date from its golden age in the eighteenth century, before the Battle of Trafalgar – fought just 20 miles off the coast – signalled the end of Spain's time as a great sea power. A long period of genteel decay followed, but new money from tourism and, of course, the influx of north European second-homers, is boosting the coffers once more and both Cádiz and inland towns like Medina-Sidonia are being spruced up.

For many, the lure of Spain is all about having a front-line, beachfront property from where you can watch the sunset over a shimmering sea. However, if you look just a few kilometres inland, you'll find more affordable property and the opportunity to become part of an authentic village community, away from the transient, seasonal nature of the coast. Historic Moorish towns

PLAYING ON THE PLAYA

Michael and Caroline Wilkins have found their ideal holiday home on the Spanish Algarve. "We didn't even know the area existed until we read about it in a newspaper," says Michael. They visited the Isla Canela property development near Ayamonte and liked what they saw, buying off-plan for £83,000.

"There's everything here we could possibly want. Our children, Thomas and Miranda, love the beach, which is quite shallow with lots of little pools for them to play in. There's also a sailing school and we've learned how to sail a catamaran. We also enjoy going to the crocodile park and the little zoo where the children can feed the animals."

Michael and Caroline love visiting nearby towns like Ayamonte, and if they want a change of scene, there's always Portugal next door. The resort can get a little quiet during the winter months, but with year-round golf and sailing, there's no excuse for being bored.

such as Arcos de la Frontera and Medina-Sidonia are gaining popularity as people realise that a modest budget can purchase a palatial *finca* or *cortijo* in the area for a fraction of the price it would be a few miles eastwards. West of Doñana, the resorts thin out, as do opportunities for buying property because building is severely restricted. But beyond Huelva, things perk up as you reach the 'Spanish Algarve'.

At its far end is Ayamonte, which straddles the estuary of the River Guadiana. As the natural frontier between Spain and Portugal, it's the hub of the Spanish Algarve and is a lively border town with old Spanish charm. Its nearest beach is around six kilometres away at the purpose built Isla Canela resort, which together with the new Costa Esuri development, just north of

Ayamonte, forms the bulk of the area's property opportunities. Here, a beachfront, three-bedroom penthouse apartment will cost over £275,000, but a two-bed apartment can be yours from under £140,000. Within these complexes, buyers have the choice of new-build town houses, apartments or duplexes. Further east towards the city of Huelva are the smaller resorts of Isla Cristina, Islantilla, El Rompido and Nuevo Portil.

Homes on the Spanish Algarve are likely to be good value for money, though some will find the area a bit too quiet during the winter. Indeed, since the Spanish tend to take all their holiday in August, for the other 11 months of the year you may find you have the beach to yourself.

IN BRIEF

Nearest airports: Jerez, Gibraltar, Seville and Faro

Main city: Cádiz

Language: Castilian Spanish

Climate: Hot in summer, with temperatures regularly above 40°C, but cooled by the Levante wind that crosses the Straits of Gibraltar, and the Atlantic breezes. Winters are mild but windy.

Not to be missed: Vejer de la Frontera, a Moorish, walled, white town, its original narrow winding streets clearly showing its Islamic origins. The sweeping white beaches at Tarifa and Bolonia, hangouts for kite- and windsurfers. The Doñana National Park, covering 50,000 hectares of dunes, heath and pine woods. Each autumn, 300,000 birds arrive on their annual migratory routes. The park is also a sanctuary for lynx and wild boar.

THE ISLANDS

Whether you enjoy dancing until dawn or an early morning cycle through pine forests and banana plantations, Spain's Balearic and Canary Islands have everything to offer.

As if mainland Spain didn't have enough riches, her two island archipelagos, the Balearics in the Mediterranean and the Canary Islands out in the Atlantic, off the coast of Africa, are a beautiful bonus. Unsurprisingly, the two groups of islands are radically different from each other, both in geography and climate, and equally, each island is different from its neighbour. Taken all in all, they complement each other beautifully and offer a complete range of holiday and home-owning options to suit any budget.

In the Balearics, the Mediterranean makes for a hot summer but a cooler winter, whereas the seven Canaries – the 'Fortunate Islands' as the Romans called them – enjoy a warm climate all year round.

Of the Balearics, Mallorca is the rich man's playground having thrown off its lager-lout image in favour of swanky shopping and multi-million euro villas that attract residents like Claudia Schiffer and Michael Douglas. Ibiza may be party central during the summer, but in winter has a relaxed, laid-back ambience. Menorca is relaxed all the time, with more fiesta

Above The inviting clear sea off Mallorca

days than anywhere else in Spain and clusters of cool white houses among the forested hills and rich red earth. The Canary Islands, on the other hand, are volcanic, the last eruption being over a hundred years ago. Again they offer something for every taste, including lively nightlife alongside fascinating volcanic landscapes. Some of the islands are agricultural (bananas are the big Canarian crop), some have strong Latin American influences, while others boast excellent windsurfing conditions and a deep sea that is ideal for big game fishing. Everywhere, the people are friendly and the authorities keen to attract foreign buyers.

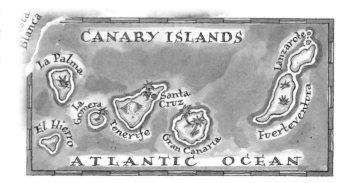

THE BALEARICS

In recent years these islands have transformed themselves from package holiday destinations to exclusive Mediterranean hot spots. No wonder celebrities love them...

MALLORCA

Seeing the changes that have taken place on the island of Mallorca over the past few years, you could be excused for thinking it's been the subject of an enormous TV makeover show. Out have gone the Union Jack shorts; in have come Gucci and Armani. In truth, Mallorca was always classy – popular with the Spanish aristocracy who holiday there each summer, and with stars such as Errol Flynn and poet Robert Graves.

As recently as 10 years ago the beautiful, unspoiled central plain and the less popular eastern coast were full of ruined farmhouses hidden in the hills. Not any more. Mallorca is now one of the most desirable addresses in Europe and you'll struggle to find any sort of property for under £100,000.

Half of the 640,000 resident population of Mallorca lives in Palma. The city is easy to find your way around and awash with

---

IN BRIEF

Main airport: Son Sant Joan Airport in Palma

Main city: Palma

Language: Mallorquín (a dialect of Catalan) and Castilian Spanish

Climate: Hot in summer, with temperatures averaging 24°C. Winters are mild, often up to 22°C in the daytime, but can be chilly in the mountains dropping to 11°C.

Not to be missed: In Palma, the cathedral is the highlight, together with the shady alleyways of the old city and the flower-filled Passeig de la Rambla. The bohemian village of Deià is the prettiest of many in the island's north-west, while the Palma to Sóller train is a fun, photogenic route through the mountains.

cultural events, shops and restaurants. For those who can afford £500,000 or so, behind the tight alleyways of old Palma are splendid apartments with cool, leafy courtyards. But on the outskirts, for example in the Santa Catalina district, there are also pleasant affordable apartments. On the fringes of Palma, you'll find the more family-oriented resorts of Magaluf and Palma Nova.

The western tip of the island is always popular with home-buyers, especially around the pretty port of Andratx, but the rocky northern coast is inaccessible and environmental laws ban new building. The ports of Sóller and Valldemossa are two of the highlights of the island.

With nowhere to build new homes, Mallorca is very much a seller's market which is why it is so much more expensive than the mainland. For an attractive four-bed villa with private pool and good sized garden, you should expect to pay around £350,000.

One of the great advantages of Mallorca is its size and geographical variety. Few places are more than an hour's drive from the airport, which has constant flights from every corner of Europe. No surprise then that it makes such a popular winter break and long-weekend destination for north Europeans.

SCRUMPTIOUS MALLORCA

Mandy Van Zuydam moved to the Balearic island of Mallorca two years ago along with her husband Simon and two daughters Jade and Kara.

"Having a place in the sun certainly does make you popular," says Mandy, "or maybe that's just the enhancing effects of my sangria!"

With their lush garden in Es Capdellá full of fruit trees, there's no better place to enjoy a jug of sangria brimming with fresh fruit.

The kids love Mandy's fresh fruit smoothies, while Simon is fond of the home-made chutneys, poached pears, figs grilled with grappa and many specialities that Mandy has had time to make since leaving the rat race behind.

So while Simon is slaving away (he has a career that enables him to work from home) Mandy and the girls are enjoying life in the sun.

MENORCA

Menorca is the second largest of the Balearic Islands and very different from its two neighbours. At under a fifth of the size of Mallorca, it has avoided the excesses of tourist development. It also has a pleasant, easy-going atmosphere compared to the frenetic pace of 24-hour Ibiza. Crime is virtually non-existent on Menorca and the locals are friendly.

The island is just 50 kilometres long and 15 kilomtres wide, with a coastline of 190 kilometres that includes 120 beaches. Particular features are the architectural remains of the 4,000-year-old Talayot culture and the Albufera d'es Grau wetlands that prompted UNESCO to declare the island a Biosphere Reserve in 1993. That means there can be very little building, leaving the rolling green countryside and picturesque villages unspoiled. It's still perfectly possible to find an empty beach in a secluded cove.

For much of the eighteenth century, Menorca was under British control, and many legacies of that time remain, not least the Georgian architecture, sash windows and dairy cows. Nowadays the British make up the bulk of visitors, and nearly three out of four foreign property buyers is British.

The capital of Menorca is Maó, in a natural harbour on the eastern coast. It has a population of 22,000, out of a total island population of around 75,000. The harbour is an exceptionally attractive place to stroll at any time of the year, and to sample the fish dishes in the numerous restaurants.

At the other end of the island is Ciutadella, the former capital, which has less British influence than Maó both historically and now. It has an interesting cathedral and

IN BRIEF

Main airport: Maó (spelt Mahon in some guidebooks)

Main city: Maó

Language: Menorquín (a dialect of Catalan) and Castilian Spanish

Climate: Always hot in summer, occasionally chilly in winter. Beware the Tramuntana wind.

Not to be missed: For wonderful views take the winding road to Mount Toro, while for wildlife and woodland walks try S'Albufera des Grau. Villages like Es Migjorn Gran have streets that are a step back in time.

Above Menorca has many pretty bays and coves: this one is Calan Porter

is famous for it St John's Day festivities in June, which include jousting. The north coast of Menorca is rocky and largely unsuitable for building on, though there are marina developments at Port Addaia and Fornells. The south is generally tourist territory and best avoided for people who are looking to enjoy the island all year round.

All this leaves most property buyers hunting in the same areas. For more economical properties look on the western side – away from the airport – at Los Delfines and Cala en Blanes. In Maó, older properties with their sash windows and English-style doorknockers are much sought-after and cost in excess of £170,000, but small apartments cost from just £70,000, cheaper than Palma. The difference, however, is the shortage of amenities in Menorca. Although the airport receives 3 million passengers a year, there are far less options on budget flights, and while Mallorca has 15 golf courses, Menorca has only one. For many, though, that's a plus.

IBIZA

Ibiza is famed for its hedonism and nightlife but, like its neighbour Formentera, it also offers the tranquillity of rolling pine-covered hills and hidden coves. Ibiza has over 200 kilometres of breathtaking coastline framing unspoiled, hilly countryside crammed with olive groves, vineyards and fields of almonds and melons. It also has probably the wildest nightlife in the world. But get away from the clubs and you can enjoy a rural idyll of tiny whitewashed villages and sheep bells tinkling amongst the orange groves.

The main centre is Ibiza Town, a maze of

medieval buildings. At the other side of the island, but only 15 kilometres away, is San Antonio. These are the main clubbing centres and properties aren't cheap. The advantage, however, is in the rental value during the summer months. Young clubbers doesn't necessarily mean poor clubbers and a property in Ibiza Town can be rented out for as much as £2,000 per week. That means even those who prefer a quieter life may rent out their property in the summer and live for the rest of the year on the proceeds.

Outside of the towns, new development is being restricted. A recent hot spot was in the south-west around Cala Jondal and Es Cubells, but the unspoiled northern tip is now up-and-coming. The off-season attractions of the island include a lively expat scene and beautiful scenery. For many, the winter is the best time to live here. A decent two-bed apartment will set you back upwards of £140,000 and you can expect to pay over £240,000 for a three-bed villa.

FORMENTERA

This small island is the getting-away-from-it-all option. The beaches are simply some of the best and most unspoiled in the entire Med, but with a population of just 5,000, you may feel a little like you are living in a village.

There is no airport on the island but catamarans and express ferries cross between Ibiza and Formentera during the day. The islanders tend to keep conservative hours so expect to eat before 10pm and drink up at 11pm.

There are few new developments but farms and village houses occasionally come on the market.

MAP

THE CANARIES

The Canaries are the UK's second most popular overseas holiday destination and the islands' contrasts ensure that if one is not quite right for you, the chances are the next one will be.

TENERIFE

The largest island of the Canaries, Tenerife's natural beauty is dominated by the volcano Mount Teide. On each side, below the moon-like *caldera* (crater) and the miles of pine forests, the northern and southern coasts are very different. The island's capital, Santa Cruz, is in the north, surrounded by banana plantations, while the south plays host to the holiday resorts. Tenerife has 350 kilometres of coastline, much of it golden sandy beaches but with a few black beaches, too. Outdoor activities like climbing, caving, hiking, cycling and water sports are becoming increasingly popular on Tenerife. For golf enthusiasts, the par 72 Golf Las Américas club is considered to be one of Europe's best courses.

Property-wise, Tenerife's most popular holiday-home towns are Los Cristianos, Las Américas, Adeje, Puerto de la Cruz and Los Gigantes. Of all the islands, Tenerife has the most properties for sale. A flat in one of the livelier resorts like Playa Paraíso will cost from £40,000. A three-bed villa at the same resort will go from £200,000.

IN BRIEF

Main city: Santa Cruz

Climate: The north of the island is slightly cooler than the south but even in winter the temperature stays around a warm 20ºC; in summer it reaches 30ºC in the south.

Not to be missed: A visit to Mount Teide is well worth the drive through miles of ancient lava flows, then a cable car ride to the top. A walk down the gorge of La Masca is a treat for the fit, followed by a cooling swim.

Above A sunset view of Arrecife harbour in Lanzarote

LANZAROTE

Lanzarote is the most volcanic of the Canaries. Internationally renowned artist César Manrique lived here and is largely responsible for the attractive look of the place. Supported by the government, Manrique shaped planning policy so that to this day it includes a ruling that no building may be more than three storeys high. Today, 90 per cent of new homes are built in cubist form, and Manrique-inspired landscaped gardens pay witness to his good taste. There are three main resorts: Puerto del Carmen, Costa Teguise and Playa Blanca. Puerto del Carmen was the first resort and is a firm favourite with tourists, making it a property hot spot for those looking to let out their home. House prices and rental yields are the highest in the Canaries.

IN BRIEF

Main city: Arrecife

Climate: Temperatures hover at 20ºC in winter and around 30ºC in summer.

Not to be missed: Visit the lava landscapes; wander the old town of Teguise; swim from black beaches.

FUERTEVENTURA

Fuerteventura was a late starter in the race to attract overseas buyers, but has used that to its advantage, ensuring controlled, environmentally sensitive growth. There are just 70,000 residents – and a similar number of goats – spread out over an island 100 kilometres long by 40 kilometres wide. Most people live in the capital, Puerto del Rosario, which has a Latin American feel, while amongst the tourists, the British traditionally stay in the north around the bustling town of Corralejo, with the Germans in the south and the mainland Spanish, who make up half of holiday-home owners, spread throughout.

The main attractions of Fuerteventura are climate and tranquillity. With winters of around 20°C and hot summers cooled by the Atlantic breeze, this island is the perfect escape from the cold of the British winter. The breeze can get up a bit – Fuerteventura means 'strong wind' – and the 150 beaches feature on the world windsurfing scene. The landscape is beautiful but stark, with blinding white sand dunes created from Sahara sand.

The property market is booming, with prices going up 80 per cent over the past five years, and areas like Costa Calma and La Pared are attracting families, retirees and investors alike. Property on Fuerteventura is still among the Canaries' most competitive, however, and an average apartment costs just over £100,000. Fuerteventura is now also attracting marina developments.

Left The wide open beach of Las Canteras in La Palma

Above right Typical whitewashed cubic buildings in Fuerteventura

Main city: Puerto del Rosario

Climate: Windy most of time, which results in an average annual temperature of 21ºC.

Not to be missed: Use those strong breezes for windsurfing and sailing, or stroll the dunes of Corralejo.

GRAN CANARIA

Gran Canaria's trade winds and mild ocean currents give it an average annual temperature of 24°C, perfect for enjoying the beaches, golf courses and stunning scenery. For a smallish dot in the ocean (just 60 kilometres long by 54 kilometres wide), Gran Canaria has a tremendous range of terrain – 128 beaches, pine forests, deep ravines and dormant volcanoes – and a microclimate that enables bananas and coffee to grow.

Gran Canaria's modern airport is 16 kilometres from Las Palmas, the cosmopolitan capital. The resorts of Playa de Maspalomas and Playa del Inglés are at the party end of the island, but quieter options include fishing villages such as Puerto de Mogán, on the southern coast. Property prices average at around £120,000 for a two-bed apartment and £200,000 for a three-bed house.

IN BRIEF

Main city: Las Palmas

Climate: Annual temperatures fluctuate between 18ºC and 25ºC.

Not to be missed: The bars of Las Palmas at night and the beaches of Playa de las Canteras by day.

LA PALMA

La Palma is the greenest of the Canary Islands and is popular for its tremendous hiking routes amid lush vegetation. It has little in the way of wild nightlife unless you're into astronomy, in which case the clear nights offer such good views of the stars that the island is home to a large scientific community. As well as the world's biggest telescope, La Palma boasts the world's largest volcanic crater, La Caldera del Taburiente, which is just a short walk from the centre of the capital, Santa Cruz de la Palma.

Just 706 square kilometres in total, and with a population of only 80,000, La Palma is also known as La Isla Bonita, because of its natural beauty. As the island still lags behind the other Canaries in attracting tourists and expats, most of the employment is in agriculture and fishing but Santa Cruz has some beautiful architecture and an interesting café society.

La Palma is one of the wettest of the Canary Islands and so will never be the first choice destination of British buyers looking for a house in the sun. Like El Hierro, the island has no mass tourism.

LA GOMERA

La Gomera is a small island, with a total population of only 18,000, and it is largely undeveloped. Most locals live in Agulo, Vallehermoso, Valle Gran Rey, Santiago and the capital, San Sebastián. Places worth a visit include Playa de Santiago, a small fishing village with a good beach, San Sebastián, where Christopher Columbus made a stop on his way to America, and

Vallehermoso, La Caleta and Santa Catalina for the beaches. The island is also home to a UNESCO World Heritage site, the Garajonay National Park, which has ancient laurel forests. The island is a popular day out for holidaymakers in Tenerife and so can get overrun with tourists.

Building is greatly restricted on La Gomera, in order to preserve the island's natural beauty. Consequently, the property market is still developing but there are great-value properties to be found.

EL HIERRO

El Hierro is the smallest and westernmost of the Canary Islands, with a population of just over 8,000, most of whom work in agriculture. Apart from being misty and rural, its rocky coastline and volcanic landscape have held it back from mass tourism, as has its isolation, though it is becoming popular with walkers and divers. At just 287 square kilometres, it is known as La Isla Chiquita (the 'Little Island').

Highlights include the Bay of Golfo, which formed following an earthquake that saw almost a third of the island disappear into the sea 5,000 years ago; the capital Valverde; Tamaduste, an old fishing harbour and small resort; and the ruins of Albarrada.

Largely undeveloped and unspoiled, El Hierro is a haven for walkers and nature lovers, seduced by the meadows of the Nisdafe plateau and the rocky coastline of Punta de Salmor.

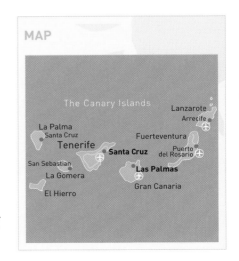

MAP

The Canary Islands

La Palma
Santa Cruz
Tenerife
Santa Cruz
San Sebastian
La Gomera
El Hierro

Lanzarote
Arrecife
Fuerteventura
Puerto del Rosario
Las Palmas
Gran Canaria

INLAND SPAIN

Away from the coast you'll find high mountain ranges
separated by valleys with rushing mountain streams, sweeping
sun-bleached grasslands and dry-as-dust plains.

T he numbers say it all. England has a population of around 50 million squeezed into 130,000 square kilometres; Spain has 40 million spread out in an area four times bigger. This is a large and relatively empty country just waiting to be explored. Over the last 40 years, many Spaniards have left the rural inland towns and villages and followed the jobs and money to the cities. For those who can take or leave the seaside, these rural areas offer outstanding property bargains and a way of life that is hard to beat. Perhaps the most famous exponent of this lifestyle is Chris Stewart in his bestseller *Driving over Lemons*. By going off the beaten track, he discovered a jaw-droppingly beautiful valley that was in many ways unchanged since the Moors left 500 years ago. His book has encouraged many to look for a similar lifestyle in Spain.

The most popular rural areas for British buyers are inland Andalusia, Extremadura, and Aragón. In fact, Teruel, in Aragón, was named by Amanda Lamb as the "seventh best place in the world to invest."

If city life appeals, the large towns have had huge amounts of public money lavished on them, and the infrastructures have been improved by EU grants. A pad in Madrid or Barcelona will cost a huge sum, but with budget flights now serving so many Spanish cities why not choose a flat in Granada, or Zaragoza? You'll find plenty of shopping and nightlife, and a great sense of community.

Left A pretty whitewashed town, typical of inland Andalusia

ANDALUSIA

Andalusia is a huge region with stunning mountains and traditional white villages. There are three major cities – Seville, Granada and Córdoba – each with its own long history celebrated in *fiestas* that can last days or even weeks. Andalusians are known to be a wilder, more passionate bunch than their northern compatriots, reflecting the heat perhaps, and this is manifested in bullfighting, horse racing and flamenco.

The range of inland properties on offer is huge. You can choose anything from a rundown *finca* (smallholding) in the Alpujarras or a *cortijo* (farmhouse) in the Sierra Nevada, to a cave home carved out in the eighteenth century, a classic expat-style villa overlooking lakes such as Viñuela, or a three-storeyed town house in a Moorish whitewashed village.

Although estimates suggest that a third of new buyers in Spain are specifically looking for a rural idyll, prices still drop as you move inland. As a rough guide, a comparably sized 'first string' property – up to 25

Above The spectacular sight of the Alhambra Palace, Granada, backed by the Sierra Nevada

kilometres inland – will cost a third of the price of a similar coastal property, while 'second string' properties – 25-75 kilometres inland – can be as much as 50 per cent cheaper. First-string villages and towns include Alhaurín, Coín, Monda, Álora and Casares; second-stringers include Antequera, Ronda and Iznájar. These are all accessible by main road from Málaga and the coast.

Those looking for a rural property should spend time exploring beyond the obvious places. The area around Lake Iznájar, an hour north of Málaga airport (known now as the Andalusian Lake District), is becoming popular.

The Alpujarras are still a popular choice, but the market is more mature here and many ruined farmhouses have been snapped up and converted. Be aware that planning restrictions are tight. The further inland you are prepared to go, the cheaper prices get and right now the Lecrín Valley, near Granada, is well worth considering.

EXTREMADURA

Extremadura, tucked away in the western-most corner of Spain and bordering Portugal, has always been one of the country's poorest and least visited regions. If you're looking for beautiful scenery and fresh mountain air, this is the place. Extremadura is divided into two provinces: Cáceres to the north and Badajoz in the south.

Cacereños have always fancied themselves as having a more aristocratic image than their country-bumpkin southern neighbours, but Badajoz creates most of the region's wealth. Extremadura is an important winemaking area but is probably better known for the famous Pata Negra ham, cured from dark-skinned Iberian pigs that feed exclusively on acorns.

Even the Spanish seem to know little about Extremadura and still believe it's a backward land of intermarriage and odd village customs. But the area has now become an important tourist attraction precisely because it's untouched and is like the rest of the country was some 40 years ago.

The people are not yet jaded by tourists, traffic and construction, and locals still greet you with a smile. There is little crime, food and drink are cheap and the weather is good.

Compared to Spain's traditional hot spots, property prices in Extremadura are reasonable. Average prices are just 43 per cent of Spain's national average, making them the lowest in the country. British-run estate agents have started opening up in towns like Zafra, something unheard of even a few years ago, and prices should continue to rise.

Just how cheap is property? Well, £25,000 will buy you a village house while a large villa with land will cost around £170,000. In comparison, there is little worth buying on the Costa del Sol for under £170,000.

But while it is possible to snap up a small house with land on the edge of a village and within a short distance of some local life, British buyers may find a lack of social life in Extremadura. Some buyers have been known to sell up due to feeling too isolated.

IN BRIEF

Andalusia: Spain's hottest region with afternoon temperatures soaring well over 40ºC in summer. Winters can be cold but snow rarely falls except on the high ground. The countryside is intensively planted in olive and almond trees, while the major cities of Granada, Seville and Córdoba combine ancient centres built by Romans and Moors, added to over the intervening centuries, with large suburbs. Andalusians tend to be hot-blooded but friendly, with tastes for bullfighting, horse-racing and hunting.

Extremadura: This often underrated corner of Spain may be hot and harsh in summer but it is also beautiful and increasingly popular with tourists and home-buyers alike. There are patches of green in lush areas like La Vera. There are mountains that offer skiing in the winter, occasional Roman remains and charming, unspoiled towns including Trujillo and Cáceres, home of the conquistadors.

Aragón: The Pyrenees offer skiing in winter – when it snows even on the low ground – while camping is popular in summer. For those looking for an authentic Spanish experience, the properties are amazingly cheap. Teruel is famous for its Mudéjar architecture.

ARAGÓN

If anyone tells you that Spain is 'spoiled', point them in the direction of Aragón, a land as far removed from the fleshpots and manicured lawns of La Manga as it is possible to get.

We know the region through Catherine of Aragón, the daughter of Ferdinand and Isabella and first wife of Henry VIII. In those days this was a thriving and rich kingdom, but the following five centuries haven't been kind and though the three provinces that make up Aragón – Huesca, Zaragoza and Teruel – are nearly ten per cent of the land area of Spain, they have only just over a million residents. So serious has been the drain of people and money that a few years ago locals started protesting that they were a forgotten backwater and the *Teruel Existe!* campaign began. At least one person was listening because, as we know, Amanda Lamb put Teruel seventh on her list of best places in the world to buy property!

In the north, Aragón forms a border with France along the Pyrenees.

> *"The Spaniards may see Teruel as a forgotten backwater but Amanda Lamb named it seventh on her list of best places in the world to buy property"*

There are ski resorts for winter and hiking trails for summer, and rural tourism is a possibility for house-hunters, though property is hard to find and will require time, patience and plenty of chatting to locals in bars and at markets. South is Zaragoza, the capital of Aragón, which stands on the River Ebro, Spain's greatest river. The city was founded by the Romans, (who named it Caesar Augusta, later corrupted to Zaragoza) and is a beautiful place to be. Spain's greatest painter, Goya, was born here, and elsewhere in the region, Opus Dei, the Catholic organisation made infamous in *The Da Vinci Code,* was founded here.

Further south, Teruel is the forgotten backwater of Spain that's gaining popularity. For decades, Brits have been drawn to rural corners of France to renovate isolated farmhouses and enjoy the local lifestyle, but those who moved to Spain were expected to prefer new-build apartments or villas, fish and chips and golf. Well, not any more, and an area like Teruel is perfect virgin territory for those seeking a challenge. Do bear in mind though that it does get very cold here in winter, and there is little in the way of transport infrastructure or other expats.

If all this sounds ideal to you, you might also like the fact that Valencia and Madrid are under two hours' drive away. House prices are excellent with village houses at around £30,000 and *fincas* varying from £15,000 for a ruin to £150,000 for a renovated *cortijo*. For those wanting to get away from it all, this is the place.

NORTHERN SPAIN

From the lush mountains of Galicia to the rugged coves of Cantabria and the snow-capped Picos de Europa, this is a place apart.

The Spanish are skilled at coming up with snappy slogans to name their attractions; hence Costa del Sol (Sunny Coast) and Costa Cálida (Warm Coast). But whoever came up with the name Costa Verde (Green Coast) shot himself in the foot – no doubt a foot encased in a green wellie – because now a land of gorgeous beaches, snow-capped mountain ranges, art, culture and fishing is known for one thing – rain! True, it does rain more here than in the rest of Spain, but it is far from being the defining feature of a land on the same latitude as Tuscany and the south of France.

The coast stretches for nearly 800 kilometres from the border of France round to Portugal and takes in the Basque Country, Cantabria, Asturias and Galicia. Popular with Spanish and French holidaymakers, North-west Spain is still largely undiscovered by the British, despite direct sea routes to Santander and Bilbao from Portsmouth and Plymouth. Now the budget airlines have become involved, with flights from Stansted to Bilbao (easyJet), Oviedo (easyJet) and Santander (Ryanair), the area should open up to us a little more. There are many attractions here such as Bilbao's Guggenheim, the surfing beaches in Mundaka and the restaurants in San Sebastián, but the region is mostly famous for its stunning geography. In the Pyrenees, the melting snows create a thousand tiny streams and waterfalls, watering verdant valleys perfect for rural tourism. Those streams make their way through Catalonia, Navarra and La Rioja, where warm weather encourages the production of Spain's most famous wine. The Basque Country is Spain's most populated and industrialised region, and comes with an entirely different language *(Euskara)*. There are lovely retreats to be found, and many fans of the area praise the food, the chalet-style homes, the local ski slopes and the easy access to France.

Moving into Cantabria you might be excused for thinking you've arrived in Ireland. To the west, the Picos de Europa seem to be harsh granite peaks from a distance but get up close and they are magical, misty places. You can still find wolves and bears here. In the villages there is a culture of bagpipes and cider, the latter poured from a spectacular height in spit-and-sawdust bars.

Finally, in the north-west corner of Spain is Galicia. Here the cities of La Coruña and Vigo are wealthy from shipping, while the region's major town, Santiago de Compostela, attracts pilgrim hikers every year. Anyone looking for golf, mega-discos and a 'full English' should look elsewhere, but the sun is starting to shine on the attractions of Northern Spain, and this area could be an excellent investment.

CATALONIA

Nestling under the protective shadow of the Pyrenees, Catalonia is a popular spot for British buyers. They came first to the beaches of the Costa Brava or for weekends in Barcelona, but soon began straying into the countryside and found a perfect land of meadows and valleys, lakes and waterfalls. For skiers there are the mountains and for swimmers there are the ice-cold lakes or the warm Mediterranean. Shoppers will love the Catalan capital Barcelona with its Ramblas and designer-shop streets; clubbers will revel in the wildest nightlife in Spain; culture vultures will appreciate the surrealist works of Gaudí and Dalí.

Catalonia is all within 90 minutes' flying time of London thanks to a range of budget options to Barcelona, Girona or Reus (near Tarragona). There's also the sleeper rail service from Paris. The housing market is relatively mature but, as always in Spain, delve a little deeper and you'll be rewarded. There are still bargain properties out there.

LA RIOJA

Known mainly for its wine, Rioja is Spain's smallest autonomous region with just 50,000 people, most of them working in agriculture. The land is kept watered by the mighty River Ebro as summer temperatures soar to 40°C. It attracts few tourists other than those on the pilgrim route to Santiago de Compostela, which passes through the north of the region, and the main city of Logroño, a stop-off on wine tours.

If lots of excellent red wine and few tourists sounds like heaven to you, then you'll enjoy exploring this area with its rolling countryside, sleepy villages, *bodegas* and farmhouses.

Above Nájera Monastery in the Rioja Province

There are properties to be found in modern, prosperous Logroño or in the wine trade centre of Haro, with village houses from £35,000 and occasional renovation projects among the vineyards – a number of independent *bodegas* have been bought out by big businesses. There's no airport here but the closest, Bilbao, is only a 90-minute drive away.

NAVARRA

Here at the western end of the Pyrenees, the peaks are lower and the lowland pastures that little bit sweeter for the huge numbers of cattle that live here. Navarra is only half the size of Wales but has a clear north–south divide, the northerners are more Basque and nationalistic in outlook while the southerners are more Castilian and loyal to Spain.

Both parts of the region are attractive to second home-buyers, though, as Navarra combines all you could want from Spain, except for a beach. Property prices are low, the countryside is beautiful, the infrastructure is good and the people know how to party – just check out the San Fermín festival in Pamplona. There is no international airport yet, but there are good rail links through France with the interchange at Irún. The closest airport is at Bilbao.

CANTABRIA

Peaceful Cantabria provides a genteel and pastoral respite from its neighbours to the east and west – the Basque Country and Asturias. It is centred on the town of Santander, served by budget flights via Ryanair and a ferry port.

Cantabria is notable for two features – the stunning coastline with its miles of sandy beaches and the Picos de Europa mountain range. The coast is particularly popular with *Madrileños* and French tourists (Jean-Paul Sartre, no less, described the village of Santillana del Mar as "the prettiest village in Spain"), while the mountains attract walkers of all nationalities, some tempted by the remote chance of encountering wolves and bears. For those looking for a renovation challenge there are opportunities inland and old farms with land can be found. However, be aware that renovations are heavily controlled and rules restrict the use of new materials, so you

"Peaceful Cantabria provides a genteel and pastoral respite from its neighbours to the east and west – the Basque Country and Asturias"

really will have your work cut out. The other benefit of this stretch of northern coast is that the people speak Castilian Spanish rather than Basque or Galician *(Gallego).*

ASTURIAS

There are a number of similarities between Asturias and Wales, and not just because the Prince of each is waiting for their chance on the throne. When Prince Felipe of Asturias goes 'home' he finds a land of mountains and valleys leading down to a seaside of craggy shores and sandy coves. As in Wales, heavy industry is slowly giving way to tourism, and the government is keen to promote the growth of rural tourism. This campaign in Asturias was boosted by the opening of Asturias airport at Oviedo to budget flights from Stansted. The future looks bright for this little green gem on the Bay

Above Boats bob in the calm waters of Baiona harbour, Galicia

Previous page The spectacular open coastline of the Costa Verde, Asturias

of Biscay, and those looking for a holiday home will find properties at half the price of those on the northern Mediterranean coast and without all the tourists. A three-bed village house in a reasonable state can be had for under £100,000. Gijón and Llanes are good places to start looking.

THE BASQUE COUNTRY

This area, known in Spain as *Euskadi*, isn't at first an attractive prospect to those seeking a place in the sun as it is Spain's industrial heartland. But prompted by the stunningly stylish Guggenheim museum in Bilbao, there is an air of rebirth about the place and the Basque people are keen to tidy up the towns and cities, clean up the rivers and promote the positive aspects of the ancient Basque culture.

Just how ancient is this culture? One clue is their language, which is the oldest in the world – dating back to the stone age – and is totally unrelated to any other (though it is perfectly possible to learn). Almost everywhere, street and road signs are in Basque and Castilian. The jewel in the Basque crown is San Sebastián, a picturesque and expensive seaside town with superb beaches. Property here is much sought-after but is cheaper inland where Swiss-style chalets can be found. The transport links with the UK are terrific, with the rail hub at Irún, budget flights to both Bilbao and San Sebastián and ferry routes, too.

GALICIA

Galicia in the far north-west is remote and battered by the Atlantic, and has a long seafaring history. The Galicians (the *Gallegos*) have a real way with seafood and produce superb marine cuisine; they love a drink, too, perhaps because of their Celtic heritage and the fact that it rains a lot! More controversially, this traditionally poor area has tended to boost its wealth with smuggling, and as a conservative region with no heavy industry it has tended towards ultra-conservative politics – it was the birthplace of General Franco.

The regional capital is Santiago de Compostela – the end of the road of the Camino de Santiago pilgrimage – and Pontevedra and Lugo are other charming stone towns. Inland, Galicia is green and forested in eucalyptus. The coasts are craggy with spectacular sea views, and there are some charming fishing ports where small-scale fishing still surivives. House prices are still some of the lowest in Spain and are rising less steeply than elsewhere. You can fly to Santiago from Heathrow with Iberia.

MAP

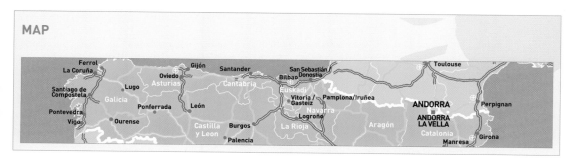

SPAIN'S CITIES

Spain's major cities never fail to amaze with their range of architecture, culture, language and lifestyle. In short, they're a colourful reflection of Spanish diversity...

W hatever else they are, Spanish cities are all, without exception, utterly individual. There's Barcelona, unbeatable for its style; Madrid, home to three of the world's finest museums, plus Real Madrid FC; Seville, the essence of Andalusia and spiritual home of flamenco; modern Valencia, venue of the America's Cup 2007; edgy Bilbao with its Guggenheim; and spell-binding Granada, the Moorish capital.

Spanish cities are never endless suburbs of homogenous housing estates. It is rare for a Spaniard to travel more than 15 minutes to work, so the long queues of traffic that plague many British towns are unheard of in Spain. In Madrid, the population lives in the city. Evenings see the streets crammed full of people enjoying what they call *'la marcha'* – life out on the town – and every hundred metres there's a little square complete with cafés and bars. It's normal to see a whole family of three or four generations enjoying an evening meal at their local pavement restaurant at midnight, all together.

Apartments in Madrid, Barcelona or Valencia can be expensive depending on the area, but only compared to the rest of Spain; they're still much cheaper than London. A two-bed designer-decorated flat in central Barcelona would cost around £250,000. For that you get shopping to die for, nightlife that will exhaust you before you exhaust it, and a sense of community that will just force you to join in.

Left Where the action is: Madrid's bustling Gran Vía at dusk

MADRID

Some great cities of the world can be crowded, dirty, overwhelming places. Madrid isn't one of them. It's a capital city that works like clockwork with few traffic jams, an efficient tube system, buses that run on time, and clean pavements. No wonder you see the people smiling in the streets.

They do say that Madrid isn't so much a city as a *pueblo* that's grown. It has that small-town feel to it, perhaps because it is pretty small in city terms, but also because it feels so manageable. You can walk from famous site to famous site, and every 100 metres you'll find an attractive square with a fountain, a couple of bars and some interesting shops. It benefits, too, from a local population that lives in the city rather than commuting into it. This results in a 24-hour lifestyle and far less congestion and pollution than is normal for a capital.

Madrid has many world-class art galleries and museums but its greatest cultural prize is the Prado, which holds a collection of art that includes

> *"Madrid is not so much a city as a pueblo that has grown – every 100 metres you'll find a square with a fountain, a couple of bars and some interesting shops"*

works by Goya, Velázquez and El Greco. It also has the wide green space of the Retiro Park, the magnificent Palacio Real and the huge pedestrianised Plaza Mayor. If it doesn't have a cathedral to match Barcelona's Sagrada Familia, then it has a temple to football – the Bernabéu Stadium – home to Real Madrid and the greatest collection of footballers in the world.

The usual criticism of Madrid is its climate, which is one of extremes. It was a modest town set on a high plateau in 1561 when King Felipe chose it to be the capital because it is at the exact geographical centre of Spain. However, its position on an elevated plain means it suffers cold, dry winters and anvil-hot summers. The *Madrileños'* response to the latter has been to take *siesta* to the max.

There are, of course, places to avoid and areas that will appeal to some more than others. Malasaña, for example, is an arty, bohemian area of bars and cafés. Similarly Chueca is a lively place full of hip boutiques where trendy bars and nightclubs are busy until the early hours.

For all these benefits of Madrid, residents must pay a high price, with accommodation taking a staggering 56 per cent of their average income. Recent rises have priced accommodation at around £2,000 per square metre, by far the highest in Spain.

Above left The elegant facade of Madrid's Royal Palace

IN BRIEF

Madrid is shopping heaven. Label lovers should head to the Salamanca district, bargain hunters to the El Rastro flea market. The Prado art museum is well worth a visit as is Real Madrid FC's Bernabéu Stadium.

BARCELONA

It's Spain's trendiest city and the epitome of Spanish sophistication, and last year it won the European Cities Monitor Award for the best quality of life in Europe. Barcelona is located on the coast of north-eastern Spain and is home to sandy beaches and sunshine for much of the year. The ski resorts of the Pyrenees are just an hour's drive away.

To these attributes, add the beautifully preserved medieval quarter, the Barri Gòtic (Gothic Quarter) and the chic nineteenth-century Eixample district, home to works by perhaps the world's most exciting architect, Gaudí. Then there's the shopping, the modern marina and the mile-long Ramblas brightened by rows of flower stalls.

IN BRIEF

Architect Antoni Gaudí left his mark all over the city, his masterpiece being the Sagrada Familia temple. Excite your senses with a trip to La Boquería food market, followed by a stroll down Las Ramblas and through the Barri Gòtic. Enjoy the sea air with a boat trip.

Left The beach at Sitges – a lively summer haunt of Barcelonians

Historically, the city is the proud capital of Catalonia, once a separate kingdom, which has long sought independence from the rest of the country. This long-held enmity is a legacy of the Civil War that saw Republican Catalonia overrun and suppressed by Franco's Nationalists, governed from Madrid.

Some claim that Catalans can seem distant and reserved to outsiders, although they are outgoing and lively with friends and family. Certainly they are hard working people – they provide 25 per cent of the country's wealth – but go to one of their wild carnivals and you'll soon see them let their hair down!

Weekends in Barcelona have become so popular with Brits that many of us are thinking of buying a flat there, not least for renting out to like-minded compatriots!

Prices here are slightly cheaper than Madrid at around £1,900 per square metre and it is one of the few places in Spain where older property is higher priced than modern. For those UK house buyers who would like to live in Barcelona, areas of the city popular for people with school-age children include the exclusive neighbourhood of Pedralbes and St Gervasi de Cassoles, located at the foot of Tibidabo district which rises into the hills that form the backdrop to this beautiful city.

A PERIOD HOME

Clare Nelson, 45, is an Irish architect living in Barcelona who specialises in renovations. She and her translator husband Graham have three children. "I live in an old block of flats in Ciutat Vella in the Gothic Quarter," she says. "I would recommend buying old property in the city centre.

"There is much more character than the modern buildings and the area is a much more vibrant place to live. There are more small shops and a more cosmopolitan mix of people. I love the village atmosphere." Clare also praises the quirky, one-off boutiques and wonderful little antiques shops of the Gothic Quarter.

Clare and Graham bought their flat for €48,000 in 1991 and have spent €6,000 on interior renovations. "Old flats need a lot of work," she says. Repairing the façade, stairway and roof and installing a lift cost the 27 owners a total of €288,000. "Our share was around €18,000," she says.

ORANGE APPEAL

Vince and Sharon Whiting talked for a long time about moving to Spain, but it was in December 2003 that they finally put their car on a ferry and drove out there. After checking out the Costa Blanca they decided to look further north and fell in love with Valencia. "It's an amazing place, with a wonderful atmosphere. Temperature-wise it is very similar to California – hence all the oranges," they say.

As keen sailors they are particularly looking forward to the America's Cup, which is being held here in 2007, but their favourite mode of transport is motorbike and they find the roads around them are excellent, though to cope with Spanish drivers Sharon says they "have to chill and go with the flow." They now plan to buy another house and rent out their own. Their biggest piece of advice to would-be Valencians is to make sure they use an established estate agent!

VALENCIA

In October 1957, Valencians looked out onto a devastated city. The River Turia had flooded. What they couldn't have known then was that this disaster would sow the seeds of the rebirth of this ancient city, Spain's third largest, as the river was diverted to prevent further flooding. The old river bed saw the regeneration of the city and was transformed with parks and exciting buildings created by the world's most cutting-edge architects, not least Valencian-born Santiago Calatrava.

And the old town is now enjoying a new lease of life too. Until recently its ancient buildings were falling into disrepair and an air of dereliction hung over the narrow medieval streets. But as Valencia has grown in confidence, so young Valencians are now clambering to buy run-down properties and transform them into bijou residences. Clubs, bars and restaurants attract a chic clientele and there's a real buzz to the place.

Valencia is a city by the sea, with Blue Flag beaches and a wonderful temperate climate. It was once the power base of El Cid, adventurer and warlord, who held it as his personal fiefdom and defended it against Arab attackers. He was no Crusader though, and switched sides to serve the Moorish

Above Valencia's futuristic City of Arts and Sciences

King of Zaragoza. As the Moors were never expelled from the city, that Arab heritage still permeates local customs, lifestyle and food.

Valencia conserves many of its ancient customs and festivities, which the locals have integrated into present-day pageantry. The famous Fallas fire festivities from 15th to 19th March are the best-known example.

When it was announced that Valencia has been chosen to host the America's Cup in 2007, house prices shot up by 17 per cent overnight. The reputation of the area has been tarnished by stories of expropriation but after intervention from the EU, this is now being resolved.

IN BRIEF

Check out the Baroque architecture, the best examples being the Plaza de la Virgen, the Palacio del Marqués de Dos Aguas and the cathedral. In stark contrast, visit the new futuristic City of Arts and Sciences, home to Europe's biggest aquarium.

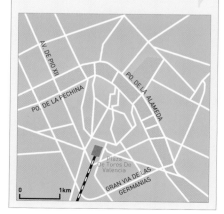

BILBAO

Bilbao is Spain's biggest port and its fourth largest city. But like many a European port city, it saw its economy collapse in the 1980s and 1990s and had to reinvent itself. This it did with the masterstroke of the Guggenheim Museum, the striking, swirling, titanium-plated building designed to reflect the city's ship-building history. Our own Norman Foster redesigned the metro system, the renowned Spanish architect Santiago Calatrava designed a footbridge and the whole city looks brand-spanking new, rather swish, and the perfect place to enjoy Spanish culture. Not surprisingly, it is also the third

IN BRIEF

The Guggenheim Museum not only contains artistic masterpieces, but is an architectural masterpiece in itself. Take the Artxander funicular to a viewpoint above the city for some fantastic panoramic views.

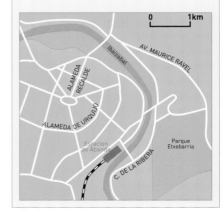

> *"Bilbao reinvented itself with the Guggenheim Museum, the striking, swirling, titanium-plated building designed to reflect the city's ship-building history"*

most expensive place to buy property in Spain after Barcelona and Madrid.

Bilbao is easily walkable. The modern city (Ensanche) stands in a loop of the Río Nervión and within this area are parks, marvellous shops along the Gran Vía, the Guggenheim and the Renfe Station. Over the bridge is the old town (Casco Viejo), along with most of the nightlife, where it is traditional to move from bar to bar amongst the Seven Streets that make up its heart. *Bilbaínos* celebrate their Basque heritage in the third week of August at the Aste Nagusia festival, which features Strong Man contests, log-chopping, hay-baling and stone-lifting; the perfect antidote to the rather more intellectual Guggenheim.

Brits have long had an affinity with Bilbao because of the importance of the city as the closest Spanish port to the UK. Indeed, British sailors founded the town's first football team. The sea route from Portsmouth via P&O has now been joined by easyJet flights from Stansted, which means that holiday home-owners in the city and its environs are just a short (cheap) hop from London.

Although expensive, property in the Basque region is not to everyone's taste as it tends to have a very distinctive chalet style. But with so much on offer, from the glories of Bilbao itself to the beauty of the surrounding countryside and the Pyrenees, it could well be worth making the investment.

Above left The Guggenheim Museum

Right Bilbao stands on the Río Nervión

GRANADA

Granada is where east meets west. Wander the city's ancient streets at dawn and you can almost hear the cry of the azan calling the faithful to prayer just as it did when the Moors ruled the city for nearly eight centuries until 1492. When they were exiled back to Africa, the Moors left behind a gorgeous Islamic legacy which includes the Alhambra Palace and the narrow alleyways of the old Arab quarter, the Albaicín. These sights are now being appreciated by a new invasion of visitors, as cheap flights from the UK bring weekend trippers and holiday home-owners keen to sample the nightlife, shopping and history of this fabulous city.

As a third of the city's residents are students, the population of Granada varies from 250,000 to 350,000 according to term time – which also makes it a good buy-to-let prospect. The large numbers of young people mean

102

"The Moors left behind a gorgeous Islamic legacy, from the Alhambra Palace to the narrow alleyways of the old Arab quarter, the Albaicín"

that the nightlife is superb, with a great mix of smoky jazz rooms and seductive flamenco clubs. The bars are plentiful and in each one the barman will quietly leave a small plate of *tapas* with your drink.

Looming over the city is the snow-capped Sierra Nevada mountain range which includes mainland Spain's highest mountain, Mulhacén (3,482 metres), and Europe's most southerly ski resort, just a 40-minute drive from the city centre. The resort offers excellent skiing from December to the May Day holiday. From then on, the sunbathing season kicks off as the beaches of the Costa Tropical are just an hour's drive away.

The pretty and unspoiled valleys of the Alpujarras are closer still and perfect for walking, cycling and horse-riding. Temperatures in winter can be distinctly chilly with frosts quite common, while summer can often see the thermometer topping 40 degrees.

With the new timetable of budget flights, buying a home in and around Granada is a good prospect. You'll find modern flats on the edges of Granada, but for something a little more unusual, you have the choice of *carmens* – homes with gardens and water features – or traditional squat little Moorish houses, which are perfect for keeping warm in winter and cool in summer.

Above left The Alhambra Palace in Granada

IN BRIEF

Visit the world-famous Alhambra Palace. Explore the ancient Arab quarter, the Albaicín, where you can drink mint tea and pick up a bargain silk scarf at the Arab market.

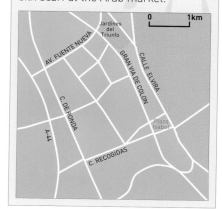

SEVILLE

In Seville you'll find a city that loves to party so much that a long-ago Spanish king invented a whole new method of drinking and dining to ensure the population was ready to work in the morning: *tapas*, little dishes served with each glass and designed to moderate alcohol flow with food. This is an intoxicating city – Andalusia distilled.

Seville seems to echo to the sounds of the bullring, and sway to the rhythms of flamenco. It's hardly surprising that Bizet's *Carmen* was set here, with its gypsy tale of jealousy and bloodlust. And in keeping with its passionate image, one Arab ruler of Seville, al Mu'tadid, had a harem of 800

women, while another earned the nickname Pedro the Cruel.

But amidst this dark passion and religious fervour, today you'll find a modern Spanish city that hosted the 1992 World Expo. It was also the first to be linked to Madrid via the 350-kilometre-per-hour AVE train, and has all the bars and cafés, department stores and boutiques that you'd expect in its larger counterparts.

Seville was also once a seafaring city; Christopher Columbus sailed from here in 1492 on his journey to discover the New World, ushering in a golden age

"Seville is an intoxicating city – Andalusia distilled. It seems to echo to the sounds of the bullring, and sway to the rhythms of flamenco"

that saw the city become one of the most prosperous in the world.

Despite a long period of decline in the seventeenth and eighteenth centuries, Seville held on to its riches until salvation came in the shape of the tourist boom of the 1970s, which has been augmented by the recent property boom. Now the nearby Costa de la Luz is bursting with activity as north European newcomers breathe life into its satellite villages. And at the heart of all this is Seville: incurably romantic, smart, sassy and so, so Andalusian.

Above Fountains in the Plaza De España

Left Seville's Torre Del Oro – Tower of Gold

IN BRIEF

Experience Seville's legendary flamenco scene in a bar in the Triana and Macarena districts. Wind down with a stroll through the gardens at the Patio de los Naranjos, the Real Alcázar and Parque de María Luisa.

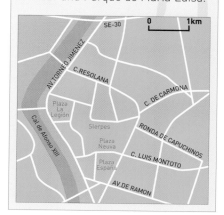

BUYING IN SPAIN

So you think you want a home in Spain? Clarifying your needs will make your property search easier and ensure you buy the home that suits you. So ask yourself some questions first...

House types in Spain are varied, ranging from newly built apartment blocks on the seafront and hillside villas overlooking the coast, to houses on *urbanizaciones* (developments) and rural *fincas* (farmhouses) in the country's interior. The best type for you will be determined by personal preference, but you must also consider how you plan to use the property and, of course, your budget.

Are you seeking a property in Spain to be a holiday home, permanent residence, retirement home or an investment? If you are buying a property specifically as a holiday home, with the aim of using the place for around six to eight weeks a year, convenience and security will be foremost. Close proximity to an international airport and local amenities such as supermarkets, restaurants and children's entertainment will be paramount; access to a beach and a swimming pool – shared or private – will be an added advantage for most people. Security and maintenance are issues, especially if you are 2,000 kilometres away in the UK, and many holiday-home purchasers prefer to buy on a gated community if budget permits, or in an apartment block that has a concierge and maintenance.

Those people looking for a permanent residence and who are of working age, particularly those with school-age children, should consider properties within easy commute of the larger cities and major coastal resorts, where most expats gravitate for work. In addition to the requirement of good local or international, English-speaking schools, practical considerations when

looking for a permanent home, depending on whether you intend to work from home or not, will be good telecommunications and utilities. Most of coastal Spain and the larger cities have broadband Internet access and mains utilities as a matter of course, but inland – often not that far from the coast – it may not be the case. Many *fincas* do not have mains electricity and water, relying on generators and pumps; telecoms can be erratic and broadband non-existent.

Retirees, depending on age, will want to consider buying in a location that has easy access to an international airport, local amenities and health facilities. It may sound obvious, but it really is worth bearing in mind that ground-floor apartments and bungalows negate the need to climb stairs. Generally, purchasing an apartment in a complex will mean that

"If you are buying a property as a holiday home, and using it six to eight weeks a year, convenience and security will be of foremost importance"

maintenance, including gardening, will be included in the management fee. Late-age retirees may wish to consider purchasing in a retirement village, where warden assistance, medical care and security services are provided.

Investors should remember the golden rules of buy-to-let. Ensure the property is no more than 45 minutes' drive from an international airport, beaches, golf courses, restaurants, bars, amenities and children's attractions. For maximum rental income, buy a two-bed property – a must for most families, who will be the majority of renters. Consider furnishing the living room with a sofa bed, too. Other considerations will be management, maintenance and cleaning between guests. A good managing agent, to whom you should expect to pay 5–10 per cent of rental income, will provide all of these services.

THE BUYING GAME

Finding and buying a property in Spain is a simple procedure once you know what you want. Here we outline some important pointers to help you with your search.

The Internet has had a huge impact on the overseas property industry, enabling you to view literally millions of properties for sale by thousands of estate agents in a matter of seconds. However, despite the resources available on-line and in magazines, most of us want to talk to an estate agent face-to-face. Many UK agents have partnered with developers or agents in Spain to offer properties for sale. Increasingly, these agents will be your first port of call but you will want to see the property you are interested in buying for yourself. Never buy a property that you haven't visited.

Traditionally, companies organise inspection trips to an area from the UK at subsidised prices – usually around £200 for a long weekend of two/three nights including flights. Inspection trips vary from company to company, some being group tours of 20 or so being ferried about in minibuses, whilst others are individual bespoke trips where you can expect to see half a dozen or more properties in a day. Stories of overly persuasive sales agents are legion, despite the industry being far less roguish than it once was. Be aware that it's easy to feel pressurised into buying a property that perhaps you wouldn't have considered had you been sitting in your living room at home.

KNOW WHAT YOU WANT

Before embarking on an inspection trip, draw up a list of requirements, with the maximum you can afford to spend at the top, and don't deviate from your list. Decide how many bedrooms you need or want. Are you looking for sea views or country scenes? Do you want a swimming pool? How far from the airport and amenities do you want to be?

Once you have drawn up your list, relay that information to the agent. Ask, and even insist, that you be given an indication of the properties they have for sale before you go. Above all, whether you are on an organised trip

or looking independently, do not sign any documents without taking advice from a solicitor.

It is never necessary to buy there and then, although to reserve a property, particularly when buying off-plan, (see page 114), it is common practice to pay a deposit in the region of £2,000–£5,000, often with a credit card. Reputable companies should offer a seven-day cooling off period. Again, do ask what the company's policy is regarding deposit amounts and terms.

FIND A REPUTABLE ESTATE AGENT

Many more of us are travelling independently since the advent of no-frills airlines and we have become more intrepid too, often venturing inland away from the costas. The vast majority of us who are not Spanish speakers want to do business with an English-speaking estate agent on the ground in Spain. Certainly in the major resorts, but also ever more so inland,

English-speaking agents are plentiful and the vast majority are reputable, honest and trustworthy.

In Spain, unlike many European countries, there is no law regulating estate agents, meaning anyone can set themselves up in business. There are, however, two professional associations, API and GIPE, whose members have sat examinations to become accredited and who are required to uphold standards to retain their membership status. These organisations have codes of conduct and a complaints procedure. In all likelihood, if you buy as you would in the UK, using professional back-up in the form of a solicitor, and you don't leave your brain on the plane, your transaction will probably run smoothly.

Your requirements for your new home will be your own, but there are a few universal truths that should help you ascertain whether you are buying in the right place before you purchase. For example, is it near amenities, road links and transport? Are telecommunications and the necessary infrastructure in place, especially important on a new-build development? It's a good idea to rent in the area you are interested in before you buy. It will give you a chance to get to know the place, and what it's like living there on a day-to-day basis, before you part with your money.

Depending on where you intend to buy, several estate agency networks operate across Spain, loosely or more formally. LPA on the Costa del Sol (www.lpaspain.com) will show you the full range of properties for sale in an area, rather than just those that were registered for sale specifically with the agent with whom you are negotiating. In Spain, similar to the UK, the seller not the buyer pays the estate agent's commission at a negotiable rate, often between three to ten per cent.

AMANDA SAYS

"YOUR SOLICITOR SHOULD CHECK THE SELLER HAS LEGAL TITLE TO THE PROPERTY AND THAT NO UNPAID DEBTS ARE ACCRUED AGAINST IT. RURAL HOMES SHOULD HAVE A SURVEYOR CONFIRM BOUNDARIES."

BUYING OFF-PLAN

In Spain during 2004, construction commenced on 761,000 properties nationwide, the highest number ever in one year, up from 680,000 in 2003. Buying off-plan means buying literally from plans, although often a showhouse or apartment may be viewed.

Buying off-plan is almost always cheaper than buying a completed property. Usually apartments are released for sale in phases, with the earlier the stage of development at which you buy, the cheaper the price. A property bought in the last phase of release will be the most expensive. However, bargains can be had towards the end of the build completion if the builder is looking to sell off the last properties before moving onto a new project, or if his end of financial year is approaching.

Depending on the construction period – often up to 18 months – and at what phase you purchase, you will have to wait to take possession. But on the plus side, payments are staged when buying off-plan, giving you time to arrange the financing and hold on to your capital longer. A typical payment structure would involve 50 per cent put down as a deposit, 25 per cent paid 6 months before completion and the remaining 25 per cent paid when the keys are handed over. There is no legislation, however, stipulating what percentages are payable when, leaving you to agree terms and conditions with the developer, or to negotiate an alternative payment plan.

Due to the rapid capital appreciation Spain has enjoyed over the past 7 years (at 127 per cent it is the highest in Europe), many off-plan buyers have found that between signing a contract of sale and taking possession 18 months later, their property has increased in value by 20–25 per cent 'on paper'. This benefit has led many estate agents to encourage buyers to purchase two, three or more properties off-plan, with the intention of selling them on prior to completion when a significant percentage of the overall payment plan is due and the property deeds change hands.

While buying and selling off-plan in this manner is perfectly legal and

many people have made a profit doing so, be aware that it may not always be as easy to sell the property prior to completion as you have been led to believe. Consider that selling a property on will effectively render it second-hand, despite it never having been lived in or even completed, and that you will have to pay an agent sales commission. You will also be competing with other agents and developers who are also selling 'brand new' off-plan properties, often with greater sales and marketing resources. Furthermore, the estate agent may well have a greater financial incentive to sell the developer's property than yours. Commission levels from developer to agent can be as high as 10-15 per cent, whereas when selling privately the average commission a seller pays to an agent in Spain is 3-5 per cent.

BUYING A RESALE PROPERTY

Buying a resale property rather than a new one is not a dissimilar process to that in the UK. Unlike in the UK, though, the asking price is generally

the price a seller expects to realise, as Spain does not have a culture of bargaining with house prices. However, the increasing anglicisation of the country has seen the practice become more commonplace.

An offer to buy is made through an estate agent, after which and upon acceptance of the offer, the process is passed into the hands of a solicitor, who should be appointed by you and not the seller, who will appoint his own solicitor (see section The Legal Process, page 122). Invariably, an estate agent will recommend a solicitor to you and they should not be viewed with any suspicion of untoward complicity, although consider that the estate agent is appointed by and works for the vendor, not the buyer. Should you have any qualms, appoint your own solicitor in the UK who will work with an associate solicitor in Spain to oversee the conveyancing processes on your behalf. See www.lawsociety.org.uk for a register of UK solicitors.

RETIREMENT COMPLEXES

Conventional resale properties and off-plan purchasing are just two means to property ownership in Spain. For those of advancing years, several retirement complexes have been built over the last decade on the Costa Blanca, Costa del Sol and Costa de Almería. They invariably have 24-hour security and are built to accommodate elderly people, with easy-to-use appliances and often with emergency alarms to local medical facilities.

CO-OWNERSHIP PROPERTIES

Co-ownership (also known as fractional ownership), not to be confused with timeshare or holiday club ownership, is freehold property ownership that enables buyers to get a toehold on the market at a fraction of the price of buying outright. Typically, ownership of a property is in quarters, sixths or twelfths, effectively making the place available for the owners' use twelve, eight or four weeks in every year. As with a freehold home purchase, size, location and amenities of the property have a bearing on purchase price. The only other thing to bear in mind is that the price may differ in certain months – it often costs more to purchase in the summer, for example.

Alternatively, many developments offer a 'rotating occupancy' policy. Effectively, four owners will buy a season. For example, Mr A buys the 12-week summer season in the first year, the autumn quarter in year two, winter in year three and spring in year four, with each of the other three partners rotating likewise. The pattern of fixed weeks or a rotating schedule is dependent on the agreement of the owners. Similarly, should one owner wish to sell, he is at liberty to sell his share either to the other owners or on the open market. Title deeds are issued and when a co-ownership is first established, a set of rules that apply to all owners is part of the legal package. Within those rules would be clauses relating to restrictions (if any) on how each owner may sell. A 'first refusal' clause is not universal but wouldn't be unusual, and it would also establish how the offer price is assessed.

BUILD YOUR OWN

An increasingly popular route to property ownership in Spain, for those with the financial means, is to buy land and build a villa. In Andalusia, the process to build may seem protracted but is relatively straightforward. Following the purchase of land sold with title deeds (your solicitor will check there is no debt on the land), an initial planning application, showing ownership where the building is to be located, should be submitted to and will be approved by the College of Architects (COA).

Once approved by the COA and once the architect's fees have been agreed, a Building Licence Application and a Certificate of Payment form (available from the local council) will be granted. The next step is to appoint a qualified architect who will draw up the outline design to meet the requirements of the owner, city planners and Spanish building regulations. The building licence (allow 2.4–4.5 per cent of the build cost figure for the fee) should then be applied for from the local council, stipulating the following: personal details of the owner; details of the proposed project; details of the architect, including college licence number; and estimated contract price to complete the planned works (excluding taxes).

Approximately 15 days to 3 months after submission, the applicant will receive notification of approval. Once green-lighted, the applicant must further provide a detailed project application and a health and safety study. Once this has been presented to the local authority registrar, applicants will receive confirmation of the final licence approval, indicating the commencement date and work conclusion. Following the hard-won battle to be permitted to build, should construction not begin prior to the stipulated work conclusion date, the council can ask for an update of the calculation of the licence fee, which could result in an increase of up to 20 per cent. Between the basic outline project and the detailed project application, the applicant has a right to make slight changes provided that they don't affect the budget costing and are within building regulations.

RESTORING AN OLD PROPERTY

At the other end of the scale, but ironically often requiring the same team of professionals, is buying a property in need of restoration or *reformas*, as it is known in Spain. If you are renovating a 200-year-old farmhouse *(finca)* don't assume that you can use modern materials to replace the old ones, as many of these older properties are built using traditional methods that are not complementary with contemporary practices. Similarly, construction materials used to build a house in the UK are very different to those used in traditional Spanish building techniques. For example, the walls in a rural Spanish property will often have been made from a mixture of straw and animal manure, smoothed over and painted. Similarly, on Ibiza, older properties had seaweed mixed in with other building materials, apparently to help keep the house sweet smelling, seaweed having an aromatic bouquet when dried. Myth or fact, when buying a property in Spain it will pay not to assume that everything is done the same way as it is in the UK.

RAISING THE MONEY

Buyers looking to finance the purchase of a property in Spain have never had more options. The question is, which one is right for you? It all depends on your plans and circumstances...

The recent rise in UK house prices has created an equity surfeit for many, enabling them to re-mortgage against their property in Britain. Those choosing to take out a mortgage on a purchase in Spain will find that most lenders, subject to status, will advance a maximum 80 per cent finance. Mortgages offered include variable rate repayment and interest-only, either in euros or sterling.

EURO OR STERLING?

Deciding whether to repay any mortgage in euros or sterling will be dependent on several factors, not least cost (mortgage rates in Spain are generally two per cent cheaper than those in the UK). Other considerations will be convenience and any charges that may be incurred by taking out a mortgage in one currency, say euros, and receiving a monthly income in sterling. In this scenario, each month the UK mortgagee would be required to transfer funds to a Spanish bank account, often incurring a fee. In addition to the fees, currency fluctuation will impact either positively or negatively, leaving the mortgagee unclear as to exactly what each monthly repayment will be. Many experts advise those taking out a mortgage currently to do so in euros, especially if they are likely to receive rental income which in turn could be paid into the Spanish bank account that the mortgagee would be obliged to open upon taking out a mortgage.

For those who have traditionally struggled to get a mortgage, such as the self-employed, self-certification mortgages, previously unavailable in Spain, are now an option. The schemes offered include variable rate repayment mortgages over 5 to 20 years at rates starting at 3.75 per cent, fixed for the first year. The loan is based on income, and can rise to 50 per cent of either the property purchase price or the valuation; whichever is lower.

CURRENCY FLUCTUATION

Those looking to pursue the self-certification option, particularly on an off-plan property, would be well advised to ensure that they do not expose themselves to 'currency risk' by omitting to take into account currency fluctuation between when they sign a sales contract and completing. The most common measure is to take out a 'forward contract' at the purchase, fixing the exchange rate to take delivery of the currency in the future. Foreign exchange (Forex) brokers offer the service between one and two years' duration, at competitive rates and most charge no commission.

THE LEGAL PROCESS

The Spanish legal system is very different to the British system and buying a property should never be undertaken without an independent lawyer. Here's how it works…

Ll too often people purchasing property in Spain take little or no legal advice and are quite casual about the purchase and the signing of legal documents. The buyer should beware because without due legal process they may find there is no title to their property, or that it was built without planning permission, both of which are serious legal issues that an independent, experienced firm of solicitors would uncover as a matter of course during the conveyancing process.

THE SOLICITOR, THE GESTOR AND THE NOTARY

Firstly, who is who in the legal chain? The solicitor you appoint, as a buyer, is legally empowered to oversee the complete sales transaction. A *gestor* (a licensed individual with certain legal powers who deals mainly with administration matters) is able to assist in preparing official documents relating to the purchase and sale of a property. A notary *(notario)* in most countries, except the UK and other common-law jurisdictions, plays a major part in the process of buying and selling real estate. The notary is an independent public official who gives professional legal advice to either the buyer or vendor and who checks that both parties understand and agree with the contents of a contract. It is the notary's function to put on the public record the fact that the title deed recording the sale/purchase has been signed in his/her presence. If the notary makes any checks as to the status of the property in question, they are usually very limited. Prior to the signing of the title deeds in front of the notary, what should a buyer consider when deciding to make an offer to buy a property? The most important thing is that you should *never* sign anything until it has been checked by your solicitor. If you do sign you will be committed to a contract that you may not understand, that may be unfair or unsafe and that could be financially structured in a way that is totally unsuited to you and tax inefficient.

PUTTING DOWN A DEPOSIT

Sometimes you may feel that you have no option but to sign some form of document in order to secure the property, particularly if you are on a weekend inspection trip. This could be one of three things: an official offer to buy the property, a reservation contract or a preliminary contract.

The official offer to buy the property is a formal letter of offer. If the seller accepts your offer this creates a legally binding obligation to proceed. You will usually, at this point, pay a small deposit of around five per cent of the value of the property. This option is relatively rare.

A reservation contract takes the property off the market for around two to four weeks during which time your lawyer can make all the necessary checks on the property. You pay a reservation fee of, typically, £2,000–£3,000. If you do not proceed because of a legal problem, you should be contractually entitled to the return of your deposit – though this is not always so and, even if it is, getting the money back can often prove difficult. If you do not go ahead simply because you have changed your mind, you will usually lose this deposit. If you do go ahead, then this deposit is treated as a part payment of the price of the house. A preliminary contract *(contrato privado de compraventa)* is a full contract to buy the property that binds you to the purchase, whatever you might find out later. When you sign this

preliminary contract you are likely to be asked to pay a preliminary deposit. This is typically 10 per cent of the price of the property, though it can be more. If this situation arises then – whatever type of document you are being asked to sign – you should have the proposed contract faxed or emailed to your solicitor *(abogado)* for comment. Most solicitors advise that if you are asked to sign any of these documents to secure a property, you sign no more than a reservation contract at this stage of the process.

SIGNING ON THE DOTTED LINE

Assuming you have signed a reservation contract with your solicitor's knowledge, there is usually a period of two to four weeks allotted for the solicitor to carry out checks on the property before you sign the main (preliminary) contract. These will include ensuring the property is sold free of all charges and mortgages. After the checks are carried out, a written report setting out the findings is produced.

Provided the checks are satisfactory, you then sign the preliminary contract and usually pay a deposit of 10 per cent of the price on a resale property and a down-payment in the region of 30 per cent on a new off-plan property. In the case of a new property bought off-plan, there usually follows a series of stage payments as the construction process progresses. Once the property has been finished (or, in the case of a resale property, as soon as everyone is ready to proceed) the final contract/deed of sale (*escritura de compraventa*) is signed in front of the notary.

Note that the seller and the buyer are usually required to attend in person to sign the documentation. However, if this is inconvenient, arrangements can be made for a power of attorney to be granted, enabling another person to attend on your behalf. This must be in Spanish form and signed in front of a notary. Your solicitor will prepare a power of attorney document on your behalf that can almost always be signed by you in the UK, and arrange for an associate in the area where the sale transaction is taking place to act and sign the title deeds on your behalf.

FEES AND TAXES

The next step is to pay the various fees and taxes. As an approximation, including solicitor's fees, land registry fees, notary's fees, taxes, associates' fees, and bank charges, budget for 11 per cent of the price of the property on top. If the property is priced at less than £50,000, the percentage will be higher; if it is priced more than £500,000, the cost will usually be a little lower. This total does not include estate agents' charges which, in certain cases, might be payable by the buyer although, almost without exception, it is the vendor who pays estate agents' fees.

These fees, of course, can at this stage be only the most general of estimates. Bear in mind that if a transaction does not proceed to completion, for any reason and at whatever stage, your solicitor will generally charge you an hourly rate for any work undertaken. Also, there will be additional legal charges, fees and taxes if you are taking out a Spanish

"As an approximation, budget for 11 per cent of the price of the property on top for fees and taxes. These will include solicitor's fees, taxes, bank charges, etc."

mortgage, or, for example, if you choose to buy in the name of a company.

One of the most critical considerations when buying a property is the name in which the property should be bought. The options available to you include: owning in your own name; in the joint names of you and your husband/wife or co-purchaser(s); in your children's name(s), in the name of somebody who will eventually inherit the property from you; or in the name of a limited company, whether English, Spanish or off-shore. Whichever choice you make, do not take it lightly as to get it wrong can cost you tens of thousands of pounds of unnecessary fees and taxes during your lifetime and on your death. Each option has its own advantages and your solicitor will advise on the best one for you. Lastly, be careful about putting the ownership of your Spanish property in any form of limited company as it may complicate matters at a later date should you come to sell the property. Always ensure that not only do you use the professional services of a solicitor, but that you also take specialist tax advice prior to purchasing; not to do so could be a very costly oversight.

Lastly, once you are satisfied the title deeds have been completed in the correct name, they will be presented for signing by the vendor and buyer (unless they have signed a power of attorney) in front of the notary. They will then be submitted to the land registry. Depending on circumstances, the amended deeds will take up to 12 weeks to be returned to you in person. However, as in the UK, this process is a formality and does not prevent you from taking possession of the property at a mutually convenient date for the buyer and seller as arranged by the two parties' solicitors. In the case of a resale property with no mortgage, the complete transaction will typically take about 10–12 weeks.

AMANDA SAYS

"ALWAYS USE A QUALIFIED SPANISH-SPEAKING LAWYER WHEN YOU BUY IN SPAIN. YOU WOULD USE A LAWYER IN THE UK! IT'S DOUBLY IMPORTANT SINCE IN SPAIN THE PROPERTY PROCESS IS DIFFERENT."

SHOULD YOU HAVE A SURVEY?

One factor that may affect the length of the buying process is whether or not you have a survey, or whether your mortgage company, should you have one, insists upon you having one undertaken. If you are buying an older property, any lender will almost certainly insist upon it; and, as you would if you were buying a property in the UK, it is often prudent to have the property you intend to buy surveyed for your own peace of mind. However, as many properties sold in Spain are brand new, it is often not obligatory to have a survey. Specifically with regard to buying a new off-plan property, Spanish law insists that, if a developer is selling a property before it is finished and wants to take any money from you, the buyer, he must provide a bank guarantee or similar. In the event that he goes out of business, or can't finish the project, you get your money back.

Spanish law also insists that new properties are issued with a licence that confirms the property is ready for habitation. Some developers will encourage you to take possession of the property before that licence has been issued but resist their offer as to move in prematurely may give rise to a variety of problems at a later date. For example, before buying ensure that

> *"Always ensure that not only do you use the professional services of a solicitor but that you also take specialist tax advice prior to purchasing"*

the property specification is agreed in detail with the builder and that the property will be delivered to you complete with the necessary licence to occupy it as a home. Finally, you should make sure that you are clear about what common parts – general facilities to be shared by all the owners in your complex – are included in the price and what the arrangements will be for the management and control of those facilities, and how much you are expected to pay in management fees annually.

CAPITAL GAINS TAX

Other costs to take into consideration if you are selling a property include capital gains tax (CGT), payable at a rate of 35 per cent if you are a non-Spanish resident (if you reside in Spain for more than 183 days in any 365 days you are deemed a resident for tax purposes) and at a rate of 15 per cent for residents, although they are entitled to 'roll-over' any gain into new property in Spain to avoid paying tax. Others exempt from paying CGT include Spanish residents aged 65-plus who have lived in the same house for more than 3 years; and anyone who bought their property prior to 31st December 1994.

Other taxes that the non-Spanish resident is liable for include Spanish wealth tax on all property and assets owned in Spain without any deductions; annual real estate tax (IBI); and property owners' imputed income tax. On death, Spanish succession tax is payable on Spanish assets. These can be deducted from any UK inheritance taxes payable on the same asset. Any rental income arising from your Spanish property is liable to Spanish income tax at a flat rate of 25 per cent (of gross rents) without any deductions.

ONCE YOU'VE PURCHASED

So now you've bought your beautiful Spanish property and you're ready to move in. Here's our practical guide to setting up home in Spain.

aving purchased a property, regardless of whether or not you plan to live in Spain permanently, you must apply for a fiscal number, known as an NIE *(Número de Indentificación de Extranjero)*. You can apply for the NIE yourself, or your solicitor can arrange for it to be initiated on your behalf at the same time as the conveyancing of your property. Otherwise, you can use a *gestor* (a licensed individual with certain legal powers), who, for a fee, will organise your application.

Alongside bank charges, another inescapable levy is taxes; all property owners are liable for certain annual taxes.

OPENING A BANK ACCOUNT

A *gestor* can help you open a bank account in Spain but the procedure is no more complicated than in the UK. Most banks in even small towns will have an English-speaking clerk. Of course, should you take out a euro mortgage with a Spanish bank, you will, in all likelihood, have an account opened in order to repay the loan.

You may also find it useful to have a Spanish account if you let your property, particularly if you have a managing agent who will deposit rental income into your account. Similarly, standing orders for bills can be paid from your Spanish account. Beware – Spanish banks have a reputation for high charges and slow service, with transfers from or to the UK taking several days and fees being charged.

WEALTH TAX

Wealth tax *(patrimonio)* is applicable on capital assets and includes any property owned, and is applied on all worldwide assets if you are a Spanish resident for tax purposes, or only on your assets in Spain if you are a non-resident. In reality, few Spanish residents pay wealth tax as the first €108,182

is exempt, rising to €150,253 if the asset is a principal residence. For non-residents, the tax rate begins at 0.2 per cent of the total value of assets up to €167,129. Thereafter, the rate payable rises to a maximum of 2.5 per cent on assets in excess of €10,695,996. Non-residents are required to complete a tax form annually, detailing the total value of their assets, which may be filed any time during the year. Allowances include debts against your property, for example, a mortgage. In reality, non-residents with assets, primarily a property, valued up to €200,000 will pay €400 in wealth tax annually.

IMPUTED INCOME TAX

Property owners' imputed income tax is not payable on an owner's principal residence (that is the primary home of a resident for tax purposes) but is payable by non-residents.

The applicable taxable rate is 2 per cent of the *valor catastral*, the official rated value of the property, attributed as if it were imagined income for taxable purposes at a non-resident's flat rate of 25 per cent. (The same percentage levied on all income, for example, rent earned in Spain.) For example, should a property have a *valor catastral* of €200,000, 2 per cent of the value, €4,000, is taxable at 25 per cent, resulting in an annual bill of €1,000.

COMMUNITY OF PROPERTY OWNERS

Other charges you may have to factor into the annual running costs of your property are community charges. Every property with shared facilities and areas, for example a private apartment development, will have a community of property owners, *(comunidad de propietarios)*, to cover common-area upkeep and cleaning of, for example, the swimming pool. Fees range from €300 a year up to several thousand, depending on the amenities and services provided and location of the property.

MUNICIPAL (COUNCIL) TAX

The annual real estate tax (IBI) in Spain is based on the rateable value of the property *(valor catastral)* and is paid by every homeowner regardless of residential status. The amount varies by location and property size but will be in the region of €1,000 per annum for a three-bed house in a coastal region. Unlike the previous two taxes which are declared, the IBI is charged to property owners in the form of a bill. It's best to set up a standing order at your bank in the same way that you pay your utilities bills.

GETTING CONNECTED TO LOCAL UTILITIES

In urban areas, electricity functions well and since deregulation in 2003, customers are at liberty to choose their supplier. The registration process is straightforward. Most companies let you register with them by phone or over the Internet and a passport or residence permit is required as identification. Electricity costs are generally cheaper than in the UK, despite connection fees of between €100 and €300. Most companies charge every two months, generally payable by direct debit from a Spanish bank account. Spain's national electric grid does suffer power cuts in rural areas where many properties are reliant on generators.

Mains gas is available in larger cities and towns – the remainder of the country uses gas bottles delivered to the door. For mains use, registration, connection and charges are applied in the same manner as with electricity, while those using bottles will be expected to sign a contract and pay a deposit to receive their first bottle. Thereafter, an empty bottle is exchanged for a full one for a small charge of approximately €10.

Telecommunications are widespread in Spain except in the most rural communities, and broadband Internet services are available in every city or town of note. Telephone registration can be made in person at a *Telefónica* office or over the Internet. Acceptable forms of identification include a passport, residence permit, utility bill or rental contract. Connection or reconnection of a telephone line costs in the region of €110 and bills are usually issued monthly.

Water supply in Spain is controlled by local municipalities, who charge a connection fee of between €100 and €500 depending on the property's location and ease of access. For usage, most municipalities have a minimum €10 a month charge plus VAT at 7 per cent, with bills raised quarterly. Prompt payment is demanded with water supplies summarily cut off for non-payment, necessitating a €40 fee and settlement of all bills before reconnection. Other municipal services and charges include rubbish collection, payable by individual property *(domicilio)*. Annual charges are usually in the region of €50–€150 and these will vary according to the property's location.

RENTING IN SPAIN

It's often a good idea to rent a property in Spain before you buy. That way you get to know what it's really like to live in a particular area.

F inding a property to rent in Spain involves a similar process to that in the UK. Letting agents in cities and major coastal resorts are plentiful, each having holiday and long-term rentals on their books. Most agents do not charge tenants a finder's fee – although it is not illegal to do so – rather, they take their commission from the landlord. Other reliable sources of rented accommodation are local newspapers' classified sections, city guides, magazines and free newspapers.

For word-of-mouth recommendations, it's worth visiting local British and Irish bars. They often have noticeboards advertising property to let and the bar staff may know of landlords looking for tenants. Increasingly, rental accommodation can be found on the Internet, too. Check out sites aimed at Britons or ex-pats, including www.thinkspain.com and www.idealspain.com.

Once you have found suitable accommodation, in most instances you will be expected to produce references and sign a rental contract, often in front of a *gestor* (a licensed individual with certain legal powers), that stipulates the length of the let – generally up to a one-year period but renewable for a total of a five-year period of tenancy. The contract will also state the rental amount payable (which can be increased in line with inflation annually), the manner and frequency of payment, and who is responsible for the payment of gas, electricity, water and municipal charges. It will include an inventory of furnishings, assuming the property is let fully or partly furnished, and will state any deposit paid. By law, a landlord has the right to charge a deposit against any damage to his property or possessions. A deposit of one month's rent is the accepted minimum for a long-term rental. Called a *fianza*, this can be held by a third party, although this is not a legal requirement.

The contract will, in all likelihood, be entitled *'por temporada'*, a short-term lease, as opposed to a long-term rental contract known as *'vivienda'*. There is no specific time limit past which a *temporada* contract becomes a *vivienda* lease. In any case, once the contracted time period has elapsed, the landlord is within his rights to ask you to leave with 30 days' notice (the same time period a tenant would be expected to give) or you may renegotiate an extension at an increased rental figure, or not, as the two parties agree.

Primarily for the tenant's benefit, leases of urban properties in Spain are regulated by the Urban Law Act of 1994. The new act, which has brought about several important changes to the old system under the 1964 act, applies only to commercial and domestic dwellings. One of the important items governed by the act, and relating to long-term leases, is the tenant's right to an automatic yearly renewal of the contract for up to five years. Note that the act does not apply to short-term or holiday lets and the laws governing a long-term lease depend on when the original contract was made.

The new act does not mean that tenants can never be evicted – non-payment of rent, damage to the property, and being a nuisance to a neighbour are all reasons why a landlord can seek to evict tenants. In order to evict, a landlord must obtain a court order and it is likely to be several months before a case comes to court.

Should you have cause for complaint, either on a short- or long-term let, you can complain to the tourist office, or if you are a semi-permanent resident you should complain to the consumer information office, *Oficina Municipal de Información al Consumidor*, whose remit it is to deal with consumer issues, including rental disputes and complaints.

BUY-TO-LET

Buying a home in Spain that you can rent out for part of the year is the ideal way to have your cake and eat it. Here are some tips for success.

The buy-to-let sector in Spain has risen exponentially over the past seven years, fuelling a booming housing market that has outstripped every other in Europe over the same period, except the UK and Ireland's. The recent slowdown in the UK housing market has, if anything, further buoyed Spain's buy-to-let market as British investors have looked to diversify and invest on the costas, where the greatest number of British holidaymakers visiting Spain stay.

Understanding how the market behaves is a critical aspect of a successful buy-to-let investment. The savvy landlord anticipates the next holiday hotspot, buying when prices are lowest and charging a premium lettings rate to ensure maximum rental yield (the rental annual income expressed as a percentage of the purchase price) possible with the fewest outgoings. In essence, becoming a profitable buy-to-let landlord requires business acumen and the courage of one's convictions, but it is not beyond anyone's grasp and there are several golden rules to follow that can help smooth the path.

Firstly, while buying off-plan with a possible 12- to 18-month wait for completion may be the most profitable way to strong capital appreciation, if you require an immediate return on your capital investment, off-plan will not provide the immediate rental income necessary to make your business proposition viable. Instead, buy a property that is close to local amenities, golf courses and the beach, and a maximum of 45 minutes from an airport.

WINNING FEATURES

For greatest tenant appeal, opt for at least a two-bed apartment, since most renters are families. Choosing an area that has sunshine during the UK's winter months will also help you to achieve year-round rental income. Most of Spain's southern regions have 300 fine days annually, while the Canaries enjoy winter temperatures like British summers, so consider buying here.

The next thing is to be clear about what you need to achieve. If you require hassle-free income and few maintenance issues, you may be best advised to purchase a recently built apartment on a development. For example, should there be a problem with the water or electricity, as the landlord it is your responsibility to sort it out, which is not always easy if you are two thousand miles away in the UK. Buying on a development, however, almost always includes a community charge to pay for maintenance to common areas – typically fees are fixed annually and are around £100 per month for a standard two-bedroom apartment – and the development management will invariably be on hand to take care of local problems that may arise at your apartment, for an additional fee.

Management fees in Spain are around 10 per cent per annum for finding tenants and an additional 5-10 per cent for managing the property on a weekly basis. Services you can expect for the fee include cleaning, security checks, inventory-taking after each let, collection and payment to you of income, and odd-job maintenance. Most landlords pre-agree with the managing agent that any work up to a certain financial amount, say £200, would be undertaken by the management company without the need to contact you for permission.

Of course, the amount decided upon is negotiable, as indeed are all fees payable. Be aware that management companies can charge however much they wish – there is no regulation of the industry in Spain – and that paying 25 per cent for a full service is not unusual.

To find a reputable managing agent ask the estate agent you buy from and your neighbours. Once you have appointed a managing agent, ensure you receive regular communication and payments. You are placing a great deal of trust in them and to ensure your buy-to-let property or business is profitable, you really will need to keep abreast of the finances to achieve a viable rental yield.

DOING THE SUMS

In layman's terms, the yield is the annual rental income expressed as a percentage of the purchase price of the property. For example, if you buy an apartment for £100,000 and during the course of the year your rental income is £10,000, the yield is 10 per cent. But lest you think it will have paid itself back in a decade, don't forget to consider all the supplemental costs, such as cleaning. In addition, the purchase price, marketing strategy, occupation levels and seasonal elements have to be considered when evaluating potential rental income. These variable factors will be affected by the number of weeks in each year you make the place available to let and when.

Don't forget to include weeks for your own, family and friends' use, void periods (empty weeks), and seasonal fluctuations in the weekly rent you can charge, usually known as high, medium and low weeks. Generally, in Spain, high is May–August inclusive; mid is March, April, September and October; and low is November–February.

MANY HAPPY RETURNS

Fred and Doris Watson, both in their late fifties, own a two-bed town house in Alicante. Says Doris, "It's on a small development on the edge of Arenals del Sol, a few miles south of Alicante. It sleeps up to six and residents have the use of two communal swimming pools. We paid around £89,000 for it in 2003 and spend about five months a year there during the winter and let it out for the rest of the year."

The property is a two-minute walk from the beach, shops and restaurants and a ten-minute drive from Alicante airport. "In August, peak season, we charge £400 a week rental, otherwise it varies between £200 and £350. We have no problem letting it and clients vary from young families to pensioners. We use a property maintenance company but only for key-holding and cleaning. That works out at about £100 a month. We advertise on the website www.spain-holiday.com and I also put cards in the local shops and post office."

> *"A net yield of around four to five per cent is considered viable rental income, bearing in mind you will need to achieve seven to eight per cent to realise that figure"*

TAXING MATTERS

Once all these factors have been taken into account, the income earned, known as the gross return, minus any money you may pay to a managing agent, any community charges that may be applicable (depending upon where you buy) and tax, equals the net return (or net income), and is your profit. Any income from rent received in Spain by non-residents is subject to a flat rate of 25 per cent income tax. For short-term letting, owners should obtain a form from the tourist authorities to apply for registration of their property. Income arising from renting the property must be declared and paid quarterly to the tax authorities by a fiscal representative. If you are a resident, rental income is included in your annual income tax declaration. (Residing in the country for more than 183 days in any one year deems you a Spanish resident for tax purposes regardless of your nationality.)

You may also be liable for tax on the rental income in the UK, assuming you are a UK resident for tax purposes, although a double taxation treaty between Spain and the UK means that you will usually simply pay the higher of the two tax rates.

Furthermore, even if you do not let your property, you do not escape income tax entirely. In Spain, non-residents with holiday homes and residents with a second home are obliged to pay annual imputed income tax (see section Once You've Purchased, page 131).

When letting, a net yield of around four to five per cent is considered viable rental

AMANDA SAYS

"BEFORE YOU BUY, MAKE SURE YOU'VE DONE YOUR SUMS. DON'T EXPECT TO MAKE A FORTUNE WITH A BUY-TO-LET PROPERTY IN SPAIN. AT BEST, YOU'LL COVER YOUR COSTS – AND GET FREE HOLIDAYS EVERY YEAR."

income, bearing in mind you will need to achieve seven to eight per cent gross to realise that figure. Of course, estimating the gross and net return is one thing, achieving them is another, which is why mortgage lenders seldom take into account rental income when loaning buyers money to purchase property abroad. But it can be done, providing you have bought at a good price and in a favourable location.

The second phase is the marketing of your property so that people know it is available for rent and it stands out from the competition. A good trawl of friends, relatives and colleagues often brings in half the income needed to achieve a respectable yield, and website and local advertising should garner the rest. Consider creating a website and/or place an entry or advertise on one or more of the general purpose Spanish web sites – such as www.thinkspain.com or the Spanish section of www.holiday-rentals.com.

Of course, any money you spend on advertising the property will impact on the profit, but it is a tax deductible expense. Ensure you file all receipts

"A good trawl of friends, relatives and colleagues often brings in half the income needed to achieve a respectable yield; website and local advertising should garner the rest"

for any money spent on the property, including maintenance work, marketing and advertising.

GUARANTEED RENTAL SCHEMES

Traditionally, there have been no guarantees of rental income – or very few – but times are changing with the introduction of reputable guaranteed rental schemes. While there is nothing new in guaranteed rental schemes – some agents have been offering them for years – often they have not paid out at the return at which they were advertised. Furthermore, the nature of the contracts have given individual buyers little or no redress when the payout has not been as advertised. However, in the past 18 months in Spain, several significant international companies have moved into the market, offering competitive and most importantly secure guaranteed rental income schemes. One company, Pierre & Vacances, a leading tour operator and house builder in France, has introduced guaranteed rental schemes at Bonmont Golf Club on the Costa Dorada and at Terrazas near Manilva, between Sotogrande and La Duquesa Golf Club, on the Costa del Sol.

First introduced in France in 1986, leaseback guaranteed rental schemes have proved extremely popular, encouraging companies to import the scheme to Spain. In essence, an owner buys a freehold property from the company and agrees to lease it back to them for a certain number of weeks per year. In return, the owner receives a guaranteed annual rental income at a pre-agreed amount depending on the number of weeks it is leased back. Pierre & Vacances offers a maximum of 4.5 per cent net with no personal usage, reducing to 2 per cent net if the landlord should choose to retain nine weeks per annum for personal usage. The leaseback term is for a minimum of a nine-year period, meaning that while you can sell the property prior to the end of the term, any buyer would have to take over the leaseback agreement. At the end of the nine years, you are able to sell the property or renegotiate an extended leaseback period with the management company. Otherwise, you need never even visit your asset, leaving all rental, contractual, management and service issues in the hands of the management company. Rental income is index linked, ensuring that over the leaseback period the rent rises in line with inflation, and payment is usually received quarterly or annually.

Advocates of guaranteed rental schemes point to the hassle-free benefits as vindication for their choice of investment; detractors argue that it is possible to earn a better yield on the open market (true, but in doing so there are attendant risks) and that so new is the scheme to Spain that when the initial nine-year leaseback term comes to an end, nobody can accurately predict whether the property will be likely to achieve an equivalent capital appreciation to properties in the wider market place. Time will tell.

LIVING IN SPAIN

What is it really like to live in Spain? If you have visited as a tourist, you will already be familiar with its different pace of life. Here's our guide to help you settle in smoothly...

It begins with a *chocolate con churros* in a local café. As you dip crunchy rings of fried dough into thick hot chocolate, watch the sun hit the pavement outside and the bougainvillea sway in the warm breeze, you know that another perfect day has started in Spain.

The appeal of Spain lies in its diverse natural beauty of mountains and varied coasts. The people, too, are varied: southerners are known for their quick wit and sense of humour, while Catalans are said to be somewhat dour and hard-working until you get to know them – then they will show you their other, fun-loving, face. It is these differences, together with the different nationalities and ethnicities that make up the population, that have created a vibrant cultural melting pot, particularly in the major cities of Barcelona, Valencia and Madrid.

Spain has kept the best of old Europe while embracing new art, architecture and technology. The Spanish are a courteous people and still hold dear a respect for the family as an institution. Many small shops are still family-owned and children are welcomed wherever they go. At the same time, the culture is modern and cutting-edge – in the towns and cities, you

"As you dip crunchy rings of fried dough into thick hot chocolate and watch the sun hit the pavement outside, you know that another perfect day has started in Spain"

can expect to find trendy shops and boutiques, exciting nightlife and great dining out. In fact, Spanish chefs such as Ferran Adriá have made an international name for themselves by creating some of the most exciting cuisine in the world.

The Spanish lifestyle is alfresco and relaxed – it has to be, because of the climate – with lazy afternoons and late nights. The people love to celebrate and party, and every village has its own fiesta. There's a real sense of community in Spain and you'll be welcomed; despite a proud patriotism, few European people have been more open and willing to befriend newcomers. This has led to a thriving cosmopolitan attitude, especially among the young who seem to love diversity and alternative lifestyles.

The Spanish love to be outdoors and to be sociable and days often end with an evening *paseo* (promenade) along palm-lined ramblas or a promenade with maybe a chilled *fino* in a pavement café – salud to Spain!

PERMITS AND VISAS

If you plan to live or work in Spain, there is little red tape for you to worry about. But there are certain legalities you need to be aware of.

IMMIGRATION, PERMITS AND VISAS

The free movement of workers within the EU became effective on 1 January 1992, which means Spain can no longer refuse a residence card *(tarjeta de residente comunitario)* to any UK citizen, or their family members and dependants. It is not a legal requirement for an EU citizen to obtain a residence card but it may be beneficial to do so to live and work in the country (see section Working in Spain, page 168).

In Spain, everyone is required by law to carry a means of personal identification at all times, which must be shown to a policeman or other official on request. A British passport will suffice, but many people find it easier to simply apply for the residence card on moving to Spain. Once applied for, it can take between one week and three months to receive the actual card.

APPLYING FOR A RESIDENCE CARD

An application form can be downloaded from the Interior Ministry website at www.mir.es. The form should then be taken to the local provincial police station *(Comisaría de Policía)* or Foreigners' Office *(Oficina de Extranjeros)*. You may be required to show a number of documents to prove your identity, including: a full valid passport; NIE (tax identification number); four passport-sized photographs; bank statements; and proof of residence,

> *"In Spain, everyone is required by law to carry a means of personal identification at all times, which must be shown to a policeman or other official on request"*

such as a utility bill. Your application will be processed and you will be notified that you can collect your residence card from the office where you made your application. Non–EU citizens will need a visa to live in Spain, and a work permit should they intend to undertake or gain employment.

PENSIONERS' ENTITLEMENTS

If you are moving to Spain for retirement purposes and you wish to claim a UK pension, you will be required to apply for Spanish residence status (*residencia*) and obtain a residence card. You are exempt from having to apply for *residencia* if you have paid into the Spanish social security system and receive your pension from the Spanish government. In this case, it is

sufficient to live in Spain with a full, valid passport. Pensioners applying for a residence card should do so at an *Oficina de Extranjeros*, providing proof of their UK pension along with the documents already detailed.

Proof of receipt of a pension may be in the form of an official letter or a statement or signed letter from a Spanish bank, documenting that your UK pension is paid directly into a Spanish bank account. Banks are not allowed to charge commission on pensions cheques.

SPANISH OR BRITISH?

You will be considered a resident in Spain for tax purposes if your major business interests are in the country, regardless of whether you also own

> *"Gaining residence status in Spain in no way means you have become Spanish. You will remain a British citizen, living in Spain."*

property and undertake business in the UK. If you own homes and have business interests in both Spain and the UK, you will not be taxed in both countries. Under a double taxation treaty existing between the two countries, signed in 1975, you will simply pay tax in the country where your major business interests lie. Gaining residence status and having a residence card in Spain in no way means you have become Spanish. You will remain a British citizen, living in Spain, unless you choose to become a Spanish citizen. Both Spanish nationals and Britons living and working in Spain enjoy the same rights to and protection within work, healthcare services, and education for their children.

BECOMING A SPANISH CITIZEN

As a British citizen living in Spain, you will not be entitled to vote in the Spanish national election. Should you wish to become a Spanish citizen, you will first have to have lived in Spain for 10 years (unless you were born in Spain, are married to a Spanish citizen, or have a Spanish parent or grandparent, in which event the qualifying period is 1 year).

Thereafter, you will be required to formally apply for citizenship and once your application is processed, you will be called to interview before a judge to demonstrate that you have integrated into Spanish society and that you are a person of good character. The judge will grant – or not – citizenship status based on your answers, references and his or her impressions of you. Successful applicants will have to swear loyalty to the King of Spain and obedience to the Spanish constitution. Further information can be found through the Spanish Ministry of Justice (*Ministerio de Justicia*). You can visit its website at www.justicia.es.

TAXATION

There's no escaping taxes, wherever you live. In Spain, wealth, property, capital gains and inheritance all have to be taken into consideration.

All resident and non-resident foreigners conducting financial affairs in Spain must have a foreigner's identification number, called a *Número de Identificación de Extranjero* (NIE). It works as both an identity card and a social security number and you need it for virtually every financial operation, including opening a bank account, dealing with the Spanish tax authorities and paying tax.

WEALTH TAX

Spain levies a wealth tax on both residents and non-residents, calculated by totalling your assets and deducting your liabilities. When calculating your liability to wealth tax, you must include the value of all your assets, including property, vehicles, boats, aircraft, business ownership, cash, life insurance, gold bars, jewellery, stocks, shares and bonds. Bank balances should be declared by producing an end-of-year bank statement showing any interest received and your average balance. If you fail to declare your total assets, you can be fined. Certain assets are exempt from wealth tax, including art and antiques (provided their value doesn't exceed certain limits), pension plans, copyrights, and assets forming part of Spain's historical heritage. Deductions are made for mortgages (for both residents and non-residents), business and other debts, and any wealth tax paid in another country. Your *gestor* will help you with this.

There's a general allowance against wealth tax of €108,182.18 per person, plus an additional allowance of €150,253 per person for their principal residence. Therefore, if your home is in Spain, you qualify for a wealth tax allowance of €258,435.18. If a property is registered in the names of both spouses (or a number of unrelated people), they should make separate declarations and are each entitled to claim the exemption. If you've bought a property with a loan or mortgage, there are deductions from your wealth tax liability. There's no allowance for non-residents, who must pay wealth tax on all their assets in Spain, which for most non-resident property owners consists only of their home. Assets are taxed on a sliding scale from around 0.2 per cent and up to 2.5 per cent on assets over the value of the allowance. Residents in Spain must make a declaration for wealth tax at the same time as they make their income tax declaration, the form being presented with payment to the regional tax office or participating banks.

Non-residents owning a single property in Spain can make their declarations on deemed letting income and wealth tax together on a single form at any time during the year, or arrange for their fiscal representative to make the declaration and payment on their behalf.

PROPERTY TAX

Property tax, which is the equivalent of our council tax, (*impuesto sobre bienes inmuebles/IBI*) is payable by both resident and non-resident property owners and goes towards local council administration, education, street and beach cleaning, social assistance, community infrastructure, and cultural and sports amenities. If the previous owner's taxes are unpaid, the new owner becomes liable. Note, however, that it is now obligatory for the vendor to produce their last IBI receipt when completing a sale in front of a notary, so this problem shouldn't arise.

It is important that the fiscal value of your property is correct, as a number of taxes are linked to this value (in addition to property tax), including deemed 'letting' income tax and wealth tax. IBI is based on the fiscal or rateable value of a property – which has traditionally been around

"In an attempt to encourage owners to rent properties rather than leave them vacant, some cities will charge double the usual IBI rates for empty properties"

70 per cent of a property's market value –
using a table of values *(ponencia de valores)*.
Values are calculated according to a variety of
evaluations, including the area of the
property, building and zoning restrictions, the
quality of the building (classified as luxury,
normal or simple), the date of construction,
and the proximity to services and roads.

The IBI rate depends on both the
population of the municipality and the level

of public services provided, and can vary considerably for similar properties
in different areas. Rates tend to be higher in resort and coastal areas than
inland areas. The basic rate is 0.3 per cent of a property's rateable value for
agricultural properties *(rústicas)* and 0.5 per cent for urban properties
(urbanas). Provincial capitals, towns with over 5,000 inhabitants and towns
providing 'special services' can increase the rate to up to 1.7 per cent.

Note that in an attempt to open up the rental market and encourage
owners to rent empty properties rather than leave them vacant, some cities
(Seville, for example) will charge double the usual rates for empty
properties.

Payment dates of property taxes vary with the municipality, and many
town halls don't send out bills, it being your responsibility to find out how
much you have to pay and when. Payment can usually be made in cash or
by guaranteed bank cheque at the tax collection office or by postal giro at
certain banks, and some municipalities accept payment by credit card. If the
tax isn't paid on time, a surcharge *(recargo)* of 10 to 20 per cent is levied in
addition to interest (plus possible collection costs), depending on how late
the payment is made. Local authorities can also levy separate fees *(tasas)* for
services such as rubbish collection, street and beach cleaning, issuing
documents, local parking restrictions and fire-fighting services.

CAPITAL GAINS TAX

Capital Gains Tax (CGT) is payable on the profit from the sale of certain assets in Spain, including property and businesses. With regard to a property, the capital gain is based on the difference between the purchase price on the deeds *(escritura)* and the sale price of a property, less buying and selling costs (and the cost of improvements), and must be declared within three months. In the past, it was common practice to under-declare the purchase price of a property, allowing the vendor to reduce his CGT liability. However, if you agree to this, when you sell the property and the actual price is declared, you will pay increased CGT.

Residents aged over 65 are exempt from CGT on the profit made from the sale of their principal home, irrespective of how long they have owned it. Residents aged below 65 are also exempt from CGT on their principal home, provided they have lived there for at least three years and plan to buy another home in Spain within three years of the sale (from the date on the

> *"Capital Gains Tax is payable on the profit from the sale of certain assets in Spain, including property and businesses"*

escritura), when they're taxed only on the amount that isn't re-invested. It is, however, important not to buy a new home until you've sold the old one, or you may not be entitled to this concession. Non-residents are taxed at a flat rate of 35 per cent. Capital gains made by residents are treated as income and limited to a maximum tax of 18 per cent.

INHERITANCE TAX

Spain imposes a tax on assets or money received as an inheritance or gift, which is paid by the beneficiaries, eg. a surviving spouse, and not by the deceased's estate, in the country where the beneficiaries have their domicile. If you're domiciled in Spain, Spanish inheritance tax is payable on an inheritance, whether the inheritance is received in Spain or abroad.

Tax is assessed on the net amount received and accrues from the date of death or the date of transfer of a gift. The amount of inheritance and gift tax liability depends on your relationship to the donor, the amount inherited and your wealth. Direct descendants and close relatives of the deceased receive an allowance before they become liable for tax. Your inheritance tax liability is calculated as a percentage of the amount inherited, from 7.65 per cent to 34 per cent, although that varies according to which region you live in.

Property can be registered in a single name, both names of a couple or joint buyers' names, the names of children (giving the parents sole use during their lifetime), or in the name of a Spanish or foreign company or trust. It is advisable for a couple not only to register joint ownership but to share other assets and have separate bank accounts, which will help to reduce their dependants' liability for inheritance tax.

HEALTHCARE

A high standard of healthcare is vital if you're to enjoy life to the full. In Spain, the national health service and private sector provide a level of care that will ensure your peace of mind.

Spain has a well-regarded national health service that works alongside the private sector. If you are visiting Spain for a holiday or short period, form E111, which can be downloaded at www.dh.gov.uk or collected from a Post Office in the UK, or the new European Health Insurance Card (EHIC), will be sufficient to cover you for free or reduced-cost emergency treatment. However, if you are a resident of Spain you should register with the Spanish healthcare system using forms E106 or E121, which will entitle you to the same cover as if you were a Spanish citizen. Pensioners living in Spain can get treatment from a Spanish doctor or hospital so long as they are registered as a resident, since the British government pays the Spanish government every year to cover the cost. On the minus side, pensioners then lose their automatic right to healthcare in the UK, becoming entitled to treatment only for problems arising when they are in the UK.

CHOOSING THE RIGHT HEALTH FORM

Anyone moving to Spain should speak to the Department for Work and Pensions (DWP) in the UK before leaving the country. Pensioners will be given form E121, which gives access to the Spanish health service for them, their spouses and any dependent children. Anyone receiving the UK Incapacity Benefit will also be given this form. Once in Spain, take the

forms to the local Spanish Social Security Office (INSS) and register for healthcare. One copy will be kept and another will be returned to the UK to await claims for healthcare from Spain. Make sure you register your form. Otherwise, you will be charged for hospital care – although you may be able to reclaim the money later.

Anyone else moving to Spain may still qualify for free healthcare for a period, so long as they have kept their National Insurance payments up to date prior to leaving the UK. They should check this with the DWP here and will need form E106, which they will need to take to the INSS in Spain to register. This form will cover those coming to Spain to work, giving them a chance to find a job and start paying Spanish social security contributions. It will only last for a limited time, and once it expires, you may need to consider private healthcare. In the past, those who divided their time between Spain and the UK fell through a gap in the system and

> *"You are allowed to choose your doctor when you go to the nearest public health centre, though in a small community there may only be one doctor"*

weren't entitled to free healthcare anywhere. However, the British government has now agreed to fulfil its obligations to people who have paid tax in Britain, and relaxed the rules to cover those who still receive a British state pension and live in the UK for at least six months of the year.

If you're employed in Spain, your employer must make social security payments on your behalf, including a deduction from your wages just as in the UK. You will receive a social security card and can register with a local doctor. The self-employed must organise their own payments, the minimum being around €240 per month, which gets them a social security card, and one for each dependent. Once you are registered and entitled to the care of the Spanish health system, you'll need to get a GP, and it's often best to ask local residents for recommendations. It may be helpful, for example, to have a GP who speaks English. You are allowed to choose your doctor when you go to the nearest public health centre *(centro de salud)*, though in a small community there may only be one doctor.

PRIVATE HEALTH INSURANCE

While emergency treatment is extremely good in Spain, waiting lists can be long for non-emergency treatment, and British people sometimes complain about the quality of aftercare. It is often a good idea to get private health insurance. Your two options are to get international cover from the UK, or Spanish cover from a Spanish insurer, who will require that you are a resident of Spain. The advantages of having private medical insurance in Spain include a wider choice of doctors and hospitals, private hospital rooms and virtually non-existent waiting lists. Disadvantages include high premiums, particularly if you're over 65. Shop around before you choose.

EDUCATION

Getting a top-class education is vital; both local and international schools have a lot to offer any family taking children to live in Spain.

There are two ways of educating British children in Spain: the local way at a Spanish state school, or at a fee-paying international or British school. The path you choose should depend on a list of criteria, such as the proximity of school to new home, whether you are happy to pay fees, the environment in which you wish your child to learn and the sort of future you envisage for them.

SPANISH STATE EDUCATION

Many British families that settle in Spain are keen to immerse themselves completely in Spanish culture. One of the best ways of doing this is to put your children through the Spanish state education system. Often, the local approach suits children who are still young enough to be able to adapt easily to a fresh environment and learn a new language, essentially infant-school age.

In most cases, by the time these children reach adulthood, they feel just as Spanish as they do British. They will have grown up with Spanish friends and they will have excellent prospects for further education and employment within Spain. For people relocating to a small village or town, getting involved with the local school can benefit parents as much as children. It is a good way to meet Spanish parents and this mixing aids the family's overall integration into the community.

As in the UK, Spanish state education is free but you do have to pay for books and materials. Catchment areas also exist: your local town hall or provincial Ministry of Education will provide lists and information about schools in your area. It is worth noting that extra-curricular activities are not high on the agenda in Spanish state schools.

The biggest hurdle for those choosing the state education route is the language barrier. Older children without an aptitude for languages may struggle in classes conducted entirely in Spanish, and consequently are forced to take extra Spanish lessons.

Making new Spanish friends can be difficult too: listen to the chatter in playgrounds of certain local schools, particularly on the Costa del Sol and Costa Blanca, and you'll hear English spoken amongst British children who prefer to stick to what they know rather than integrate with the natives.

BRITISH SCHOOLS

If keeping your child within the British education system is top of your list of priorities – and you can afford the fees – then a private British school in Spain should be your first choice. These are ideal for parents that move around the world but want their children to complete a normal UK education, or for families that intend to return to the UK without interrupting a child's education. Annual fees range from €4,700 to €10,000 (£3,160–£6,730) for boarders. Many British and other international schools also offer the Spanish school-leaving examination, *Selectividad*, which is needed for entrance into Spanish universities. Another benefit of these schools is that they provide a meeting point and social hub for expat parents. Like other international schools, British schools are open to all nationalities. In some of these schools, British pupils are outnumbered by their Spanish counterparts, sent there by their parents to receive a bilingual education and benefit from the high standard of teaching and facilities. There are now 50 British schools in Spain, more than in any other country outside the UK. Most are concentrated around Madrid and along the coast from Barcelona to the Costa del Sol.

The environment in a British school has a true international feel to it, even though the bulk of classes are taught in English and the schools stick to the UK National Curriculum, preparing pupils for SATs, GCSEs, and A-Levels or the International Baccalaureate – both of which open doors to university in the UK. The academic standard is notably high at most British schools and, as you would expect with fee-paying schools, the sporting facilities and extra-curricular opportunities offered are generally extensive as well. If you're concerned that by sending your children to a British school, you might be sending them to a little 'pocket' of Britain in Spain where they'll be sheltered from the Spanish culture, take note: it is law that British schools offer Spanish language classes and conduct certain classes in Spanish.

INTERNATIONAL SCHOOLS

British schools are not the only form of international school available in Spain. Other English-speaking schooling options include American equivalents, where pupils follow the US curriculum. When it comes to choosing an international school for your child, a good starting point is to look at those that are affiliated to professional associations. The National Association of British Schools in Spain (www.nabss.org) and the Council of British Independent Schools in the European Communities (www.cobisec.org) have codes of conduct and minimum requirements for member schools; they will be happy to offer advice and help you find the right school for your child. Once you've decided on a school, register your child there as soon as possible – many schools have years-long waiting lists.

PENSIONS

If you've always dreamt of retiring to Spain to enjoy the beautiful weather and excellent cost of living, it's easy to make your dream a reality.

If you are retired and eligible to receive a state pension in the UK, you will be able to draw that pension while resident in Spain and it will be index-linked. However, you do need to talk to your local DWP (Department for Work and Pensions) office and the Inland Revenue before you go, informing them of your intention to move abroad permanently and making sure you have all the relevant forms correctly completed.

As a resident of Spain, you are liable to pay Spanish tax on all your worldwide income and that includes your pension. The only exception is if you are an ex-civil servant, when the taxation of your pension and its collection is down to the country paying it. To ensure you do not get taxed in both countries, you can claim either relief at source from UK income tax or repayment of UK income tax by contacting the Inland Revenue direct or visiting www.inlandrevenue.gov.uk.

A state pension can be paid directly into your Spanish bank account, as can most company pensions. If, for some reason, a company pension has to be paid into a UK account, it is a simple matter to arrange a bank transfer. Banks cannot charge commission on pension cheques. The amount of state pension you are entitled to depends on whether you or your spouse have paid National Insurance Contributions (NIC). If so, you will get the standard UK rate. You can get a state pension forecast by going on the pensions

website (www.dwp.gov.uk). If you have never paid NIC, or paid very little, you will still get something but it will be much reduced, perhaps nearer half the rate for a person who has paid in full.

How often you receive your pension is largely your choice. If you are going abroad for less than two years, you can choose to have the whole amount as a lump sum when you return to the UK. Otherwise, you will be paid every four or thirteen weeks, in arrears. It will usually be paid straight into your bank or building society, either in Britain or Spain, but you can have a sterling cheque sent out to you in Spain if you prefer.

Other entitlements you should take into consideration include sickness and invalidity allowances, officially called 'special non-contributory benefits'. Generally, these benefits are not payable abroad on a permanent basis, but you can claim them for up to six months, for example if you were going for a winter break to decide if you wanted to live in Spain permanently. These entitlements include the Disability Living Allowance, Attendance Allowance and Carer's Allowance.

WORKING IN SPAIN

Many Brits who move to Spain plan to get a job there or set up a business. There are plenty of opportunities for both and rewards can be high.

Modern Spain has fully emerged from its nationalist past and embraces the modern market-led world of free enterprise with open arms. A visit to any major city, particularly the big three – Madrid, Barcelona and Valencia – will leave you in no doubt that the younger generation are entrepreneurial: fashion shops, coffee bars and artistic endeavours proliferate in many of the fashionable districts. In these multinational cities, English is the international language and most young Spaniards speak it to a high standard. Assimilation for Britons moving to Spain, therefore, is not as difficult as it once might have been in all but the most rural areas. Of course, an early adoption of the native language will pay dividends in the job market and the locals will think better of you if you try to speak Spanish. In the cities and on the costas, language schools are commonplace and many large Spanish companies, particularly in the larger cities, will provide Spanish lessons for English employees, especially if it benefits their business.

On the costas, it is largely true to say that learning the language is not a prerequisite to gaining employment. For many Britons immigrating to Spain, career opportunities revolve around the service industries, often providing a benefit to the local English-speaking community. Popular sectors – and employers of a significant number of expats – include the real

estate, hotel and catering, retail, and health and beauty industries.

Increasingly, entrepreneurial Brits moving to the area are not content with taking a job simply to make ends meet. Inspired by their new environment and spotting a gap in the local market, they are using skills gained in the UK and buying into or setting up businesses in growing numbers. At any one time, hundreds of businesses – ranging from bars to B&Bs and hairdressers to hotels – are for sale, if you know where to look. News of businesses for sale in the expat community is often passed on by word of mouth, but commercial estate agents and local newspapers are a good place to begin your search.

Official sources of practical advice include the *Ventanilla Única Empresarial* (VUE), a one-stop shop for businesses, which has a website at www.vue.es (in Spanish only) that details start-up information by sector. There are 31 VUE offices nationwide.

HOW TO FIND WORK

There are plenty of job opportunities in Spain, from
professional positions and teaching to seasonal work on the
costas – and you don't always have to speak Spanish.

I n an ideal world, anyone emigrating to Spain would only be doing so once they have secured a job there whilst living in the UK. Certainly, in the majority of professional sectors or industries where multinational companies operate, it would be unusual to pitch up in a big city and begin knocking on doors. For senior appointments, recruitment is usually undertaken at head-office level in the country where the company has its headquarters, while junior positions will in all likelihood be advertised locally in the Spanish press.

If you speak Spanish to a reasonable level, national daily papers that carry job ads include *El Pais* (www.elpais.es), *El Mundo* (www.elmundo.es) and *El Periodico* (www.elperiodico.es). Specialist job seeker publications include *Laboris* (www.laboris.net), *Segundamano* (www.segundamano.es) and *El Mercado de Trabajo* (www.elmercadodetrabajo.com). The latter features hundreds of positions vacant weekly, while *Segundamano* is published three times a week. Even if your Spanish is not great, the online versions of many of the above are also in English or can be translated with a search engine.

For more general work, several companies and non-profit making organisations, both in the UK and Spain, exist to help jobseekers find employment. A Europe-wide employment service named EURES is a network of several hundred offices across Europe linked by the online portal www.europa.eu.int/eures. The EURES network exists to provide services for the benefit of workers and employers, as well as any citizen wishing to benefit from the principle of the free movement of persons, and involves three types of service provision: information, advice and recruitment/placement (job-matching).

"The Spanish equivalent of the Jobcentre has over 700 offices throughout the country; as an EU member, you're perfectly entitled to use this service"

In Spain, on a more localised level, temporary employment agencies, known as *Empresas de Trabajo Temporal* (www.mtas.es/empleo/ett-OIA/inicio.htm) or ETTs, operate by contracting individuals and hiring them out to other companies as needs arise. Individual ETTs operating include Adeco (www.adeco.es) and Ranstad (www.ranstad.es). Another company offering individuals temporary work is UK-based Manpower (www.manpower.co.uk). The company's strict application code insists that they will only employ fluent Spanish speakers, with references, who are living in Spain at the time of their application.

There is also the Spanish equivalent of the Jobcentre, known as INEM, with over 700 offices throughout the country, and one in every major town. As an EU member, you're perfectly entitled to use this service.

WORKING OPTIONS

Translation services are always in demand by Spanish companies, increasingly appreciating the necessity to promote their services to an English-speaking market. Obviously, you will need to be fluent in both languages in order to undertake this kind of work.

Teaching English as a foreign language (TEFL), however, does not require the teacher to be a Spanish speaker. TEFL schools proliferate in all the major Spanish cities, many of them American schools that employ a broad range of native English speakers from around the world. In almost all cases, employees will need to have a TEFL qualification gained either in the UK or in Spain.

There is no official body that represents the industry but see the TEFL section of the Education page at www.guardian.co.uk for an independent guide to TEFL courses, and what is expected of TEFL teachers. You'll also find situations vacant. Those with TEFL qualifications and a specialist knowledge, for example of mechanical engineering, will find they are in great demand as English-speaking classes are not only aimed at school-age

children but at Spanish adults too, particularly in the vocational sector. It is quite common for Spanish CEOs of large companies to attend 'breakfast classes' before work. TEFL work is often poorly paid, around €1,000 (£700) per month for a 30-hour teaching week, except for private work where hourly fees of £30 or more can be achieved.

Temporary or seasonal work on the costas is normally a possibility. Visit the clubs, pubs, bars, shops and supermarkets that expats frequent and, providing you have a skill set that's in demand and the genuine desire to work, generally it will not take long to secure employment. Beware, however, that upwards of 25 per cent of all work in Spain is considered to be unofficial or 'black market' employment. As in the UK, it is illegal to work and not pay taxes (see Income Tax, page 176) and furthermore anyone working illegally will have no holiday or sickness entitlement. If caught working illegally, you may be deported from Spain.

EMPLOYMENT LAWS

There are various legal and financial factors you need to be aware of while you're searching for a job – and once you've landed one.

All resident and non-resident foreigners (including EU citizens) working and therefore conducting financial affairs in Spain must have a *Número de Identificación de Extranjero*, or NIE (see Taxation, page 152).

You can apply for it at any police station with a Foreigners' Office, getting the forms from a Spanish lawyer or via the website of the regional government of Spain in the area you intend to move to. If you have an employment contract or a letter from a Spanish employer or business stating why it requires you to have an NIE, you can obtain a number in around a week, but otherwise you may have to wait for up to three months.

In theory, and according to EU law, any trade or professional qualification awarded in the EU will be recognised in Spain. This is particularly true with public sector jobs, so for example, a British teacher can become a teacher in Spain without taking any further examinations. Similarly, crafts or tradespeople like hairdressers, carpenters or construction workers, can have their experience certified under the UK Certificate of Experience scheme. To have your qualifications recognised, you can take all your certificates, along with Spanish translations of them, and a 'transcript', or list, of all the components of the course, to the Spanish Ministry for Sport, Education and Culture in the area where you wish to work, to obtain an *'homologación'*. It costs about £100. Medical and architectural qualifications can be recognised via a simpler and faster system (see www.naric.org.uk). If you have difficulty in finding work, you are entitled to unemployment benefit (with certain restrictions), and the same Job Seeker's allowance as you would get in the UK. The Spanish INEM will pay you for up to three months, but you must first register in the UK to see whether you qualify. Once you find a job, you should take your work contract and social security registration to the central police station or Foreign Nationals Office of your region to get the EU citizen's resident and work permit *(la cuenta ajena)*. Your employer will then organise tax and payment into the social security system. There is another work permit for the self-employed *(la cuenta propia)*. On commencing work, you are entitled to a legally binding contract, but since they can be verbal or written, any disagreements might come down to one person's word against the other.

Also, since dismissing employees is an expensive business many contracts are very short term. After three years' worth of temporary contracts, the

employer has an option of letting you go or employing you permanently. If you choose to work for yourself, consider that operating as a sole trader means you will pay less tax than if you formed a limited company (see Starting a Business, page 180). Remember, too, that if you plan to operate out of business premises then you will need an opening licence.

For certain professions, including architects, lawyers, estate agents and nurses, you will also need to register with the appropriate professional organisation *(colegio)*.

INCOME TAX

There's no escaping income tax, but there is plenty of help available when it comes to completing and submitting your tax returns.

Employees' income tax *(retenciones)* is deducted at source by employers, ie pay-as-you-earn, although you must still make a tax declaration. The self-employed pay their income tax quarterly *(pago fraccionado)*.

Liability for income tax in Spain depends on where you are officially resident. As previously stated, you become a fiscal resident in Spain if you spend 183 days or more there during a calendar year, or your main centre of economic interest, such as investments or business, is in Spain.

Income tax is payable on salaries, pensions, capital gains, property and investment income (dividends and interest), and income from professional, artistic or agricultural activities. If you are a non-resident or own more than one property in Spain, your income also includes two per cent of your property's fiscal value *(valor catastral)*. For example, if your second Spanish property is officially valued at €150,000, then €3,000 must be added to your income. Your main home is exempt.

MAKING YOUR TAX DECLARATION

Those gaining income in Spain – both residents and non-residents – must lodge their annual income tax declaration between 1 May and 20 June (other than income from property letting). If you are entitled to a refund *(devolución)*, the deadline is extended until 30 June. Income tax is paid a year

in arrears, so, for example, the declaration filed in the year 2006 is for the 2005 tax year. If your earned personal income is below €8,000 for an individual declaration, then it isn't necessary to declare it. Unlike in the United Kingdom, Spanish tax returns are not sent out by a tax office. Instead, they are usually purchased from a tobacconist's for around €0.30 each, or you can obtain one from a tax advisor or from your local tax office *(agencia tributaria)*.

There are three kinds of tax declaration forms in Spain:

Abbreviated Declaration: The *declaración abreviada* is used for taxpayers whose income derives entirely from earnings or from pensions and investments that have already been subject to Spanish withholding tax.

Simple Declaration: The *declaración simplificada* is for those with the same sources of income (usually below €600,000) as for the abbreviated

declaration, plus income from letting, certain business and agricultural income, and capital gains from the sale of a permanent home where the total gain will be invested in a new home in Spain.

Ordinary Declaration: The *declaración ordinaria* is for incomes from all sources other than those mentioned above, eg business or professional activities and capital gains.

An instruction booklet is provided with the returns form, and the tax office publishes a booklet containing examples of how to complete the forms. If you can use the *declaración abreviada*, you should be able to complete your own tax form, perhaps with a little help from the tax office. However, most people require professional help to complete the *simplificada* and *ordinaria* tax forms, and your local tax office may have multilingual staff which makes it easier. Note, however, that tax offices won't help you complete an *ordinaria* tax form, and you must make an appointment in any circumstances.

Income tax for the self-employed in Spain is self-assessed and paid at the same time as the tax declaration is made. You can pay either the whole amount when the form is filed, or 60 per cent with your declaration and the balance by the following November. Tax returns should be submitted to the district tax office where you're resident for tax purposes, or they can be filed (and payment made) at designated banks in the province. Payment must be made in cash and personal cheques are not accepted. If no payment is due on a return, it must be filed at the tax office. If you delay filing your tax return by even a day, you must pay a surcharge on the tax due, although it is possible to request a payment deferral. While late payment of any tax bill usually incurs a surcharge of 20 per cent, large fines can be imposed for breaches of tax law and in certain cases forfeiture of the right to tax benefits or subsidies for a period of up to five years. The fraudulent evasion of €30,000 or more in tax is punishable by fines of up to six times the amount defrauded and/or imprisonment. You should retain copies of your tax returns for at least five years, which is the maximum period that returns are liable for audit by the Spanish tax authorities.

Unless your tax affairs are simple, it is advisable to employ an accountant or tax adviser *(asesor fiscal)* to complete your tax return and ensure that you're correctly assessed. There are 'foreign' tax assessors *(asesores de extranjero)* who specialise in filing returns for foreigners, particularly non-residents. The fees charged for filing tax returns vary and for residents are around €35 for a simple return and €60 for an ordinary return; the fee for filing a tax return for a non-resident is usually around €35. Make sure that you have your tax return stamped as proof of payment by your advisor.

STARTING A BUSINESS

If you fancy doing your own thing, here's our guide to dealing with the Spanish bureaucracy involved.

S tarting a business in Spain is essentially no different to doing so in the UK. You will need to do your market research to identify that there is a need for your services and carry out a viability study, probably by writing a business plan (essential if you want to borrow money from a bank). It will help to have an understanding of legislation – health and safety at work, employment law and so on.

Where Spain and the UK do differ significantly, however, is in the level of bureaucracy involved in starting a business. Spain is notorious for the red tape you have to overcome. Thankfully, the country is modernising and accepting the fact that its systems are antiquated and insurmountable to Spaniards, never mind to foreigners. When starting a business, in theory there should be little difference for a native or a citizen of another EU country; the reality, however, is somewhat different. While no EU citizen is required to have a residence card to live and work in Spain, it will be virtually impossible to obtain a bank loan without one, and business life will be considerably easier if you do have one.

In order to decide what legal status and business structure you wish your company to operate under, it will pay to consult a lawyer before you begin trading. The solicitor (*abogado*) will also advise you as to your legal responsibilities and requirements with regard to running a business in Spain. Lawyers' fees can vary greatly so make sure you know what your

solicitor will be charging before you engage their services. Other sources of information are the local Chamber of Commerce (www.camara.org) and *Ventanilla Única Empresarial* (VUE) (www.vue.es), a one-stop business shop.

FREE BUSINESS ADVICE

Every city of a reasonable size will have a Chamber of Commerce, and there are 31 VUEs in Spain and its islands. Their services are an invaluable source of free advice and information in areas such as business planning, labour obligations, government grants, obtaining municipal licences, and your fiscal obligations. You may need to take a translator, however, as the service is primarily set up for Spaniards.

Only you will know the type of service or business you intend to provide. However, the legal status of the business, and any applications for permits that may be required to carry it out, will have far reaching consequences should you not get them right in the first instance. For

HUNTER GATHERER

Guy Hunter-Watts owns a small B&B in the village of Montecorto, near Ronda.

He's been there since 1988 and finds work not only running the B&B but also as a writer and walking guide.

"I start my day walking down the hill to buy bread, pick up the post and dip into Diego's bar for a quick coffee."

When he arrived, Andalusia was very different to how it is now: "Women still washed their clothes on rocks wedged across the stream, and children would run up the hill to see what an *inglés* looked like, giggling at my long hair and odd manner of dress!"

Guy's farmhouse became a guesthouse organically, each room being gradually improved over the years until he had enough presentable rooms ready to start letting some out. And now that hard work has paid off and the business he created is thriving.

example, do you intend to run your business as a sole trader *(empresarios individuales)* or as a limited liability company *(Sociedad de Responsabilidad Limitida* or *SL)*? Operating as a sole trader means you will pay less tax than if you were to form a limited company. However, as in the UK, you are personally exposed to any bad debts that the business may incur, whereas if the company is limited then it and not you personally is liable for any debts.

Other considerations will be that as a sole trader, you are required to pay into the Spanish Social Security System under the *autónomo* scheme that then gives you entitlement to the Spanish Health Service.

BECOMING A SOLE TRADER

A sole trader will pay individual income tax (known as IRPF), and VAT (known as IVA). Depending on your business and whether you have premises, you may need a *licencia de apertura*, an opening licence that deems the business premise suitable for the specific commercial enterprise.

By far and away the most popular legal structure is that of the sole trader. Over two-thirds of new businesses incorporated annually choose this status. The majority of Britons operating a business that provides a

> *"The majority of Britons operating a business that provides a service and has no employees will find the sole trader structure gives them legal status while minimising bureaucracy"*

service, for example a tradesman, hairdresser or beautician, and who do not employ others, will invariably find this structure gives them legal status while minimising the bureaucracy necessary to run their business.

LIMITED LIABILITY COMPANIES

The formation of a limited liability company (SL), as in the United Kingdom, is a more detailed procedure with greater responsibilities and accounting procedures. The minimum capital required for incorporation of an SL is €3,005.06, making it a realistic choice for many small- and medium-sized companies.

Other business structures recognised by Spanish law include partnerships *(Sociedad)*, general partnerships *(Sociedad Colectiva)* and limited partnerships *(Sociedad Comanditaria)*. Each structure has its merits depending on what

"*Under Spanish labour law, an employee is deemed to have a legally binding contract, whether or not it is written down, so a verbal contract is as good as a written one*"

you are seeking to achieve and the level of personal protection you feel your business requires.

Spanish law requires that all business enterprises keep orderly accounts, including inventories and financial statements, and file them annually. Companies with shareholders must keep minutes recording any resolutions adopted. Unless you particularly wish to become familiar with the intricacies of Spanish accountancy, business and tax law, it will pay to engage an accountant *(asesor fiscal)* or a *gestor*, if your accounts are straightforward. SLs will probably require the services of an accountant experienced in company practices.

Just as in the UK, in certain cases, depending on business turnover, an audit of the company's accounts will be necessary.

REGISTERING FOR VAT (IVA)

Regardless of your business structure, size or turnover, you must register for VAT (IVA) and apply to the tax authorities for a tax identification number. For businesses with a turnover under €6 million, IVA is payable quarterly. Certain sectors are IVA exempt, including health and education. Depending on the business sector you operate in, you will also require insurance, for example building, contents, public liability, employer's liability, goods in transit, loss of earnings due to an accident or professional negligence. Seek the advice of a solicitor.

EMPLOYING OTHERS

Should you employ anyone, they are entitled to an employment contract and you are obliged to register the contract with the Spanish Institute of Employment (INEM). Note: under Spanish labour law, an employee is deemed to have a legally binding contract, whether or not it is written down, so a verbal contract is as good as a written one in the eyes of Spanish law. Employers must register the engagement of new employees with the social security authorities and make an employee's (as well as employer's) social security contribution (23.6 per cent of the employee's earnings).

COMPUTING SUCCESS

Gary and Jane Adcock moved with their children to the Costa Blanca early in 2005 and set up a franchise of a UK computer consumables company, Lasertech.

"The pace has been hectic," says Jane. "Finding a place to live, school for the kids, and setting up a business. We've discovered that it is more bureaucratic here but once you get started business is surprisingly easy."

They've been amazed at how many nationalities run businesses in Spain and their clients include Germans, Danes, Poles and, of course, Spaniards. "Although we're working hard we're really enjoying ourselves. The weather is great and the fiestas are fantastic."

Best of all, Gary and Jane like the local markets where they can buy fresh fruit and fish and have started exploring the white villages on their days off. So, is there any chance of them going back to the UK? "No chance!" they say in unison.

QUESTION TIME

From work and pensions to property laws and moving, here are some of the most commonly asked questions about buying and living in Spain.

THE BIG ISSUES

Q. Am I allowed to work in Spain?

A. Yes, as an EU citizen you are just as entitled to work in Spain as a Spaniard. But you must obtain an NIE number from any police station that has a Foreigners' Office. This can take up to three months unless you have a letter from an employer stating that you need it earlier. Your employer will then organise tax and payments into the social security system.

Q. How well will my children settle into school?

A. That depends on them and how old they are. Younger children usually find it easier to adapt and learn Spanish, and are helped in this by the schools who will organise Spanish lessons for them while the Spanish children are learning English. In some parts of Spain there are so many English families

that they are never short of English-speaking playmates anyway. There are also English-speaking nurseries and schools if you want to try those.

Q. What happens about my pension?

A. If you are eligible for a pension in the UK, then you are eligible to draw that pension in Spain and it will be index-linked. Before moving to Spain you need to contact the Department for Work and Pensions to make all the arrangements. The money can be paid into a bank account either here or in Spain. Should you decide to come back to the UK at a later date, you will simply revert to having the money paid here.

Q. What happens if I become ill or incapacitated?

A. The Spanish healthcare system is just as good as the UK's, though it is often expected that the family will take a greater part in the provision of care, especially for elderly patients. If you're in Spain for a holiday, you will be covered by form E111 for emergency treatment at no, or low, cost. But those living in Spain will need to register with the Spanish healthcare system, after which they are entitled to the same cover as the Spanish. Pensioners have the same rights as they would in the UK because our government pays the Spanish government each year to cover the cost.

Q. How does inheritance law in Spain differ from the law in England and Wales?

A. In England, a person is free to dispose of his or her estate just about how they please. Spanish law, however, states that you must leave at least two-thirds of your estate to your children or grandchildren. A person is therefore seriously limited in how much of his or her estate can be left to the surviving spouse.

BUYING PROPERTY

Q. What are the benefits of buying off-plan?

A. Off-plan, jargon for buying a property that hasn't yet been built, allows you to build a house just the way you want it. It's the equivalent of buying a tailor-made suit rather than one off the peg as you can choose the kitchen you want, the bathroom you want, etc. Not only that, but historically it has tended to mean that buyers see a rapid rise in the value of the house and can get first choice of position on a new development. The disadvantages are the potential for problems during construction and with stage payments. To avoid this, only go through a reputable company and employ a good lawyer who speaks English and Spanish.

Q. Is it easy to renovate a ruin?

A. It can be. There isn't quite the same reverence for old buildings as we have in Britain, so they can be bought for much less than new builds. There also isn't the same shortage of craftspeople, and while the rules are being enforced more, it is still fair to say that it is easier to renovate a ruin to your tastes in Spain than in this country. As ever, a good lawyer is the starting point, as planning regulations can be a real minefield in rural areas. After that, you'll need a good architect, then a builder. In some rural areas that have seen a flight of residents to the cities and the costas, there may be grants available for renovation. Check with the Town Hall.

Q. What about buying just land?

A. This method of finding a place in the sun can make sense, and make money, coming in at about 30 to 40 per cent cheaper than buying a ready-made home, but with more risk and worry. The most vital element is ensuring that the land has planning permission to be built on – moreover, enough to build a suitable-sized house. You must get this permission from the Town Hall. An architect will then be required to prepare drawings of the building for approval by the Town Hall architect's office. Your lawyer must ensure that title remains yours during building work, or an unfinished house can remain the property of a builder should problems arise.

Q. How expensive is it to build a swimming pool?

A. A pool will certainly add value to your property. For a standard eight-by-four-metre pool, dug into the ground, lined with concrete and with a tiled finish, you can expect to pay upwards of £10,000, and it will take one to two months to complete. To add a heater for year-round swimming might increase the price by some £4,000. A much cheaper alternative is for an above-ground, rigid PVC pool, which can be had for under £500 and set up in minutes. Don't underestimate the work that

needs to go into a pool, with maintenance of the pumps and filters and keeping the water clear and at the right pH. An alternative is to have the pool maintained by a specialist, which will cost around £70 per month.

Q. Are property-finding services worth the money?

A. They certainly can be but you have to be careful. Although most Spaniards have wised-up now, in the past property might be sold over a beer in a bar and the best properties never appeared in an estate agent's window. So paying for the services of a Spanish-speaking specialist with an ear to the ground and good negotiating skills was essential. But what could be nicer than someone weeding out the duff properties and only passing on the best to you, at a well-negotiated price? The downside is that they can cost a lot of money, charging an initial non-refundable registration fee and then a percentage – say, 2.5 per cent – on top of the purchase price. Others charge the homeowner. If you can, go by personal recommendation.

Q. How does the buying process work?

A. It's a reasonably straightforward procedure. First there is the signing of the private contract by both buyer and seller, where you will be expected to pay a deposit of around £3,000. Next comes the signing of the *escritura*, the official document recording the transfer of ownership, which is signed in front of the notary. That's when the rest of the money changes hands. After this, your *gestor* will register the property with two different organisations: the Land Office *(Catastro)* and the Property Registry *(Registro de la Propiedad)*. Finally a new *escritura* is issued and the buying process is then complete.

Q. How much will I have to pay in fees and purchasing costs?

A. Around 12 per cent is normal. This includes the notary's fee and purchase tax of around 7 per cent. The estate agent will generally charge 10 to 15 per cent on the sale, compared with 2 per cent in the UK. The upside is that most house purchases are completed much more quickly than in the UK.

Q. Should I use the estate agent's lawyer or find my own?

A. Would you ever buy a house in Britain using the agent's pal? Then why do so many do just that in Spain! The laws of inheritance are more complicated in Spain so it is essential that you are sure you have clear title. And for those buying off-plan through stage payments, the

solicitor will check that everything is in place before your money is handed over. You must never accept the word of a person with a vested interest in the sale of the property and always obtain independent legal advice. Why independent? Because some estate agents might have a cosy arrangement with a lawyer. You can find a lawyer in the local newspapers or through personal recommendation, and they should be registered with the *Colegio de Abogados* and be able to provide a registration number.

Q. Where can I get a mortgage?

A. You can get a mortgage either in Spain or in England, but a Spanish one is likely to be cheaper. Alternatively, you could go for an English bank operating in Spain. As a non-resident you would be unlikely to get a Spanish mortgage for more than 70 per cent of a Spanish property, and as a general rule, mortgage repayments in Spain cannot be for more than a third of the mortgagee's disposable income. Mortgages in Spain are also over 15 rather than 25 years.

Q. Are inspection trips better than going it alone?

A. If you're an independent-minded person with a good knowledge of Spain then inspection trips are probably not for you. Trips to Spain tend to focus on new-builds and off-plan, so if your heart is set on restoring a traditional farmhouse in the foothills of the Sierra Nevada, you will want to avoid them. What inspection trips are good for is seeing a wide selection of properties within a specified budget within a short space of time. Once you have briefed the trip organisers of your exact requirements, you can leave it up to them to get the most out of your four days in Spain. They will know the area and be able to advise on what property options will suit your needs. Everything, from flights to accommodation, is organised for you, but make no mistake, it's not a holiday; you'll be kept busy viewing. For those who speak no Spanish, inspection trips are an easy way of seeing properties and getting a taste for an area of Spain without the hassle of tackling any language barriers.

Q. How does buying leaseback property work?

A. When you buy through a leaseback scheme, you buy a property with a guaranteed amount of annual rental return. It works by you buying a freehold property from a company on the condition that the company rents it back from you for a certain number of weeks per year. In return,

you, the owner, get a guaranteed annual rental income at a pre-agreed amount depending on the number of weeks it is leased back. Bear in mind that the number of weeks you can use the property for personal holidays will be limited, and leaseback contracts usually last for a minimum of nine years.

Q. What are forward currency contracts?

A. Forward currency contracts, or forward time option contracts, are signed agreements that allow you to buy foreign currency, such as euros, at a fixed exchange rate for use sometime in the future. In most cases you do this through a forward currency broker. The main benefit of forward currency contracts is that they let you know exactly how many euros your pounds will buy at a predetermined date, or between two predetermined dates, in the future. This way, once you have secured a property abroad, you can then secure the euros you will need to buy it through a forward currency contract without leaving yourself open to fluctuations in the exchange rate. Think of it like this: you wouldn't buy a property in the UK without knowing exactly how much you were paying for it; why take that chance with a property abroad you are paying for in a foreign currency?

MAKING THE MOVE

Q. How do I organise removals?

A. There are many companies specialising in relocations to mainland Europe and you can find them in the *Yellow Pages* or on the Internet, or in the back pages of *A Place in the Sun's everything Spain*. They charge £4,000 to £6,000 for the contents of a four-bedroom house; less if you can be flexible over delivery times or go as a 'part load'. The removal company will normally do a survey two to three months before the move and give you a quote, so call them as soon as you have any details of moving times. They will also want to know of any potential access problems with your new property. Always ensure you are covered by insurance and you are using a reputable company, before you wave goodbye to all of your possessions!

Q. Can I take my own car to Spain?

A. You can, but you can only use it for six months of the year or less unless you are prepared to legally export it. To legally export your car, you must surrender the registration document to the DVLA who will send you a Certificate of Permanent Export (V561) to take to Spain with you. Once there, the car will need to be registered with the local transport authorities and kitted out with Spanish number plates. It will also need Spanish Road Tax and to pass a Spanish MOT (ITV).

Q. How do I take my dog or cat to Spain?

A. Since both the UK and Spain signed up to the Pet Travel Scheme (PETS), the process is straightforward so long as your pet is healthy and over eight weeks old. First, visit your vet to get your pet micro-chipped with an ID number – painlessly injected into the back of its neck – and to be rabies vaccinated. This should all cost around £180. Whether you fly, drive or go by ferry, you must ensure that the operator is willing and able to take pets, as many don't – especially the budget airlines. The process for bringing animals back to the UK is more complicated and you should seek advice from the PETS Helpline on 0870 241 1710.

Q. How do I furnish my new home?

A. For those looking to furnish a property quickly and with minimum hassle, there are several companies who will organise the whole package for you, from fridge-freezers to teaspoons, and put it all in place. They'll even make the beds for you! This will cost from £4,000 but obviously depends on the package and the size of the house.

White goods (fridges, washing machines etc) are no longer much cheaper than in the UK but it is certainly worth buying them over there in local electrical stores like Upper. IKEA is opening branches in Spain but for more of a Spanish look try going to a Spanish supermarket like Mercadona or Carrefour. And don't forget El Corte Inglés; safe, reliable, very local – and you can always find English-speaking staff.

SETTLING IN

Q. Is it easy to find a job?

A. Spain suffered badly from unemployment for decades, but in the last few years the level has fallen from around 20 per cent to just over single figures today. There is certainly pressure for jobs due to the influx of people from other countries, especially Eastern Europe and South America, and the increasing number of women in the workplace, but there is no reason for you not to expect to find a job. Of course, those who speak Spanish fluently will find it easier to get work. Professionals such as teachers and nurses can usually transfer with little effort as long as they speak some Spanish. Those who don't speak Spanish will probably be restricted to either jobs

in tourism, work in the expat community or jobs that don't involve speaking!

Q. Is the work culture different?

A. Yes. The most obvious difference is in the pattern of the working day, where businesses open later, at around 10am, and close at 1.30-ish for the siesta. People go home for a long lunch and a short snooze and then return to work at around 4pm until 7pm or 8pm. Two commutes in one day might not sound like much fun, but very few Spaniards live more than 15 minutes from their workplace so there is little travelling involved and relatively few traffic jams. Although the siesta is said to be dying out due to the global nature of work these days, it is proving to be an enduring habit in Spain, and there's no denying it's as healthy as it is popular. The Spanish also believe in a far more personal approach to business – much more than we do – so meetings might be conducted over a long lunch or an evening meal, and can seem slow compared to the frenetic pace of the UK business scene.

Q. How do I set up a business?

A. The entrepreneur is very welcome in Spain, and even in a big city you'll be amazed at how many small shops there are compared to the homogenous high streets we see in Britain. Also, there are all the new expat communities on the costas who still prefer to do business with an English-speaker, so the opportunites for plumbers, electricians, pool cleaners, dentists and so on are enormous. Registering for work is perfectly simple. The first person you will need to speak to is a lawyer, who will put you in touch with a *gestor* who will sort out the paperwork and steer a course through the red tape. It is also important to speak to an accountant who will ensure you are paying the correct amount of tax.

Q. What's the purpose of a community of property owners?

A. When you buy on a complex or urbanisation, you automatically become a member of the community of property owners for that development. It means that you, together with your neighbours, are responsible for the ownership of common property, such as lifts and stairways in the case of apartments, and gardens, communal pools and roads on complexes. You pay an annual fee for the maintenance of the communal areas so you don't have to worry about cleaning the pool, trimming the hedges and mowing the lawn. Even the exterior painting of the properties is done on

behalf of the owners on a regular basis in a great many community developments. Monthly community charges can range from £30 to £300, depending on the size and location of the development.

Q. Is Spanish difficult to learn?

A. Learning any language requires effort, patience and a certain amount of bravery. If you are learning from scratch, you'll see results immediately. It will help if you can speak some French, as a lot of the grammar follows the same patterns and there are parallels in the vocabulary. Don't worry if your Spanish is not word perfect; just making the effort will go a long way with Spanish people and you will get so much more out of life if you can converse with the locals. There is an increasingly large English-speaking expat community in Spain, but it's not true that everyone speaks English. If you're moving to a new home, speaking Spanish to local tradespeople, builders and utility companies, or those you encounter whilst setting up a business, will mean you'll get a superior service and you'll be in a better position to negotiate if things go wrong. Knowing the language also brings potential for making endless new friendships, and gaining a deeper understanding of the culture.

GETTING THERE

Want to travel to Spain but unsure of the best way to get to your destination, or where the closest airport or ferry port is? We've rounded up all the information you need...

Airport

Ferryport

ALICANTE, FROM:

Belfast	easyJet
Birmingham	MyTravel, Avro, Flybe, BMI, Excel
Bournemouth	Thomsonfly
Bristol	easyJet
Cardiff	bmibaby
Cork	Aer Lingus
Coventry	Thomsonfly
Doncaster	Thomsonfly
Dublin	Aer Lingus
Durham Tees	bmibaby
East Midlands	easyJet, bmibaby, Excel
Edinburgh	Globespan, Air Scotland
Exeter	Flybe
Gatwick	Excel, BA, Avro, easyJet, Monarch
Glasgow	Globespan, Avro, Air Scotland, Excel
Heathrow	BMI, BA/Iberia
Leeds Bradford	Jet2
Liverpool	easyJet
Luton	easyJet, Monarch
Manchester	Avro, Monarch, bmibaby, Excel
Newcastle	easyJet, Excel
Norwich	Flybe
Southampton	Flybe
Stansted	easyJet
Teeside	bmibaby
Exeter	FlyBe

ALMERÍA, FROM:

Birmingham	MyTravelLite, Flybe
Bristol	easyJet
Dublin	Aer Lingus
Gatwick	BA, easyJet, Excel
Stansted	easyJet, Ryanair
Manchester	Monarch, Excel

BARCELONA, FROM:

Birmingham	BA, MyTravelLite
Bristol	easyJet

Belfast	Jet2
Cork	Aer Lingus
Coventry	Thomsonfly
Doncaster	Thomsonfly
Dublin	Aer Lingus, Iberia
Edinburgh	Globespan
Gatwick	easyJet, BA, Excel
Glasgow	Globespan
Heathrow	BA, Iberia
Liverpool	easyJet
Manchester	Avro, BMI, Monarch
Newcastle	easyJet
Leeds Bradford	Jet2
Luton	easyJet

BILBAO, FROM:

Dublin	Aer Lingus
Heathrow	BA/Iberia
Stansted	easyJet

FUERTEVENTURA, FROM:

Bristol	Excel
Dublin	Aer Lingus
Gatwick	BA, Avro, Excel
Manchester	Avro, Excel
Liverpool	Nexus Airways

GIRONA, FROM:

Blackpool, Bournemouth, Dublin, Glasgow, Luton, Liverpool, East Midlands, Shannon, Stansted; via Ryanair

GIBRALTAR, FROM:

Gatwick	Avro, BA
Heathrow	BA
Luton	Monarch
Manchester	Monarch

GRANADA, FROM:

Stansted	Ryanair
Liverpool	Ryanair
Gatwick	Monarch

GRAN CANARIA, FROM:

Birmingham	MyTravelLite
Bristol	Excel
Doncaster	Thomson
Dublin	Aer Lingus
Gatwick	Avro, BA, Excel
Glasgow	Globespan
Liverpool	Nexus Airways
Luton	Monarch
Manchester	Excel, Avro

IBIZA, FROM:

Birmingham	MyTravelLite
Coventry	Thomsonfly
Doncaster	Thomsonfly
Gatwick	BA, easyJet
Liverpool	easyJet
Manchester	BA, Jet2
Newcastle	easyJet
Stansted	easyJet

JEREZ, FROM:

Stansted	Ryanair

LANZAROTE, FROM:

Birmingham	Avro, MyTravelLite, Excel
Bournemouth	Palmair
Cardiff	Avro, Excel
Dublin	Aer Lingus
East Midlands	Avro, Excel

FERRIES

There are two ferry routes to Spain from the UK. These are via 'cruise-ferry' to Bilbao from Portsmouth with P&O, which sails every three days (except during refitting in January), and Plymouth to Santander with Brittany Ferries. This service has two sailings a week from early March to late December.

Gatwick	BA, Avro, Excel
Liverpool	Nexus Airways
Luton	Monarch
Manchester	Avro, Excel
Also: Glasgow, Humberside, Newcastle and Stansted via Excel	

MADRID, FROM:

Birmingham	BA
Bristol	easyJet
Dublin	Aer Lingus
Edinburgh	BA
Gatwick	BA, easyJet
Heathrow	BA/Iberia, BMI
Liverpool	easyJet
Luton	easyJet
Manchester	BA, Monarch

MÁLAGA, FROM:

Aberdeen	Monarch
Belfast	easyJet
Birmingham Flybe,	MyTravelLite, Avro, Excel, BMI, Monarch
Blackpool	Monarch
Bournemouth	Thomsonfly
Bristol	easyJet, Excel
Cardiff	bmibaby, Excel
Coventry	Thomsonfly
Cork	Aer Lingus
Doncaster	Thomsonfly
Dublin	Aer Lingus, Ryanair
Durham Tees	bmibaby
East Midlands	easyJet, bmibaby
Edinburgh	Globespan, Air Scotland
Exeter	FlyBe
Gatwick	Excel, BA, Avro, easyJet, Monarch
Glasgow	Globespan, Avro, Air Scotland
Heathrow	BA, Iberia
Leeds Bradford	Jet2
Liverpool	easyJet
Luton	easyJet, Monarch,

Avro,	Jet2
Manchester	Monarch, BA, Jet2 bmibaby, Excel
Newcastle	easyJet, Avro
Newquay	Monarch
Southampton	Flybe
Stansted	easyJet, Avro, Excel

MALLORCA, FROM:

Belfast	easyJet
Birmingham	MyTravel, Flybe, bmibaby
Bournemouth	Thomsonfly, Palmair
Bristol	easyJet, Excel
Cardiff	bmibaby, Excel
Coventry	Thomsonfly
Doncaster	Thomsonfly
East Midlands	bmibaby, Excel
Edinburgh	Globespan
Exeter	Flybe
Gatwick	BA, Avro, easyJet, Excel
Glasgow	Air Scotland, Globespan, Excel
Heathrow	BMI
Leeds Bradford	Jet2
Liverpool	easyJet,
Luton	easyJet
Manchester	Monarch, bmibaby, Jet2, Excel
Newcastle	easyJet
Stansted	easyJet, Avro, Excel
Teeside	bmibaby

MENORCA, FROM:

Gatwick	BA, Avro
Glasgow	Excel
Luton	Monarch
Manchester	Avro

MURCIA, FROM:

Birmingham	MyTravel, Flybe, bmibaby

Dublin	Ryanair
East Midlands	bmibaby, Ryanair
Exeter	Flybe
Gatwick	BA, easyJet, Excel
Glasgow	Ryanair
Leeds Bradford	Jet2
Liverpool	Ryanair
Luton	Ryanair
Manchester	bmibaby, Jet2, Excel
Southampton	Flybe
Stansted	Ryanair

OVIEDO, FROM:

Stansted	Ryanair

REUS, FROM:

Dublin, Liverpool, Luton and Stansted; via Ryanair

SANTANDER, FROM:

Stansted	Ryanair

SANTIAGO DE COMPOSTELA, FROM:

Heathrow	BA, Iberia
Stansted	Ryanair

SEVILLE, FROM:

Dublin	Aer Lingus
Gatwick	Avro, BA
Heathrow	BA/Iberia
Stansted	Ryanair

TENERIFE NORTH, FROM:

Gatwick	BA

TENERIFE SOUTH, FROM:

Birmingham	MyTravelLite, Avro
Bournemouth	Thomsonfly, Palmair
Bristol	Avro, Excel
Cardiff	Avro, Excel

Doncaster	Thomsonfly
Dublin	Aer Lingus
East Midlands	Avro, Excel
Gatwick	Excel, BA, Avro
Glasgow	Avro, Globespan, Excel
Leeds Bradford	Avro, Jet 2
Liverpool	Nexus Airways
Luton	Avro, Monarch
Manchester	Avro, Monarch, Excel, BA
Newcastle	Avro, Excel
Stansted	Avro, Excel

VALENCIA, FROM:

Bournemouth	Thomsonfly
Coventry	Thomsonfly
Doncaster	Thomsonfly

Gatwick	BA, Avro, easyJet
Heathrow	Iberia
Stansted	easyJet, Ryanair

VALLADOLID, FROM:

| Stansted | Ryanair |

ZARAGOSA, FROM:

| Stansted | Ryanair |

BILBAO, FROM:

Portsmouth with P&O Ferries on the *Pride of Bilbao*. Sailings: twice weekly except January 6th to 28th, 35-hour outward crossing, Saturday evening arriving Monday morning or Tuesday arriving Thursday.

SANTANDER, FROM:

Plymouth with Brittany Ferries on the *Pont Aven*. Sailings: twice-weekly until December 22nd, leaving Sunday/Wednesday afternoon and taking 18 hours. Services resume 6th March.

PLEASE NOTE

Flights correct at the time of going to press but you should be aware that summer/winter schedules change and new routes are often added so it is always best to check with individual airlines.

AT-A-GLANCE

Aer Lingus	www.aerlingus.com	0845 084 4444
Air Scotland	www.air-scotland.com	0141 222 2363
Avro	www.avro.co.uk	0870 458 2847
BA – British Airways (inc GB Airways)	www.ba.com	0870 850 9850
BMI	www.flybmi.com	0870 607 0555
BMI Baby	www.bmibaby.com	0870 264 2229
Brittany Ferries	www.brittanyferries.com	0870 536 0360
City Jet	www.cityjet.com	00 35 318 700 300
easyJet	www.easyjet.com	08717 500 100
Excel	www.excelairways.com	0870 998 9898
Flybe	www.flybe.com	0871 700 0535
Globespan	www.flyglobespan.com	0870 056 6611
Iberia	www.iberiaairlines.co.uk	0845 850 9000
Jet2	www.Jet2.com	0871 226 1 737
Monarch	www.flymonarch.com	0870 040 6300
MyTravelLite	www.MyTravelLite.com	08701 564 564
Palmair	www.bathtravel.com/palmair	01202 200 700
P&O	www.poferries.com	08705 202020
Ryanair	www.ryanair.com	0871 246 0000
Thomsonfly	www.thomsonfly.com	0800 000 747
Nexus Airways	www.nexusairways.com	0845 257 1721

ADDRESS BOOK

Here are essential contact details and useful websites to help you to find out more about Spain and the Spanish way of life.

USEFUL ADDRESSES

Spanish Embassy
39 Chesham Place
London SW1X 8SB.
Tel: 020 7235 5555

Spanish Consulate General
20 Draycott Place
London SW3 2RZ
Tel: 020 7589 8989
www.conspalon.org

Spanish Tourist Office
22-23 Manchester Square
London W1M 5AP
020 7486 8077/ 14
www.tourspain.co.uk
www.spain.info

British Embassy in Spain
C/Fernando el Santo, 16
28010 Madrid
Tel: 00 34 91 700 82 00/
91 319 0200
www.ukinspain.com

The Federation of
Overseas Property
Developers, Agents and
Consultants (FOPDAC)
1st Floor, 618 Newmarket

Road, Cambridge CB5 8LP
Tel: 0870 3501223
www.fopdac.com

The National Association
of Estate Agents (NAEA)
Arbon House
21 Jury Street
Warwick CV34 4EH
Tel: 01926 496800
www.naea.co.uk

British Association of
Removers (BAR)
Tangent House
62 Exchange Road
Watford
Hertfordshire WD18 0TG.
Tel: 01923 699480
www.removers.org.uk

USEFUL WEBSITES

MOVING TO SPAIN
Age Concern España
www.acespana.org
Airpets
www.airpets.com
Bishops Move

www.bishopsmove.com
British Schools in Spain
www.nabss.org
DEFRA
www.defra.gov.uk/animalh/
quarantine/index.htm
European Union
www.europa.eu.int
Foundation for Foreign
Property Owners
www.fipe.org
Help in Spain
www.helpinspain.org
Inland Revenue
www.inlandrevenue.gov.uk
Pension Service
www.thepensionservice.gov.uk
Robinsons International
Removals
www.robinsons-intl.com
The British Council
www.britishcouncil.org
ExpatAccess
www.expataccess.com

MORTGAGES, BANKING
AND CURRENCY EXCHANGE
Barclays Spain
www.barclays.es

Blevin Franks Financial
Consultants
www.blevinfranks.com
Foreign Currencies Direct
www.currencies.co.uk
Banco Halifax Hispania
www.halifax.es
HIFX
www.hifx.co.uk/spain
Moneycorp
www.moneycorp.com
Mortgage4Spain
www.mortgage4spain.com
Sterling Exchange
www.sterlingexchange.co.uk
Travelex
www.travelex.co.uk

CONVEYANCING AND TAX
Blakemore Walker
www.blakemorewalker.com
HOME
www.homecostablanca.com
John Howell & Co Solicitors
www.lawoverseas.com
Marbella Solicitors
www.marbellasolicitors.com
Michael Soul and Associates
www.spanishlawyers.co.uk
Puerta Vides
www.puertavides.com
RICS
www.rics.org/spain
SCF Group
www.scfgroup.com
The Rights Group
www.therightsgroup.com

NEWS, CULTURE AND
GENERAL INFORMATION
About Spain
www.aboutspain.net
All about Spain
www.red2000.com

British Expats
www.britishexpats.com
Catalan Life
www.catalanlife.com
Costa Blanca News
www.costablanca-news.com
Escape to Spain
www.escapetospain.com
Euroresidents
www.euroresidentes.com
Expatica
www.expatica.com
Ideal Spain
www.idealspain.com
In Madrid
www.in-madrid.com
In Spain
www.in-spain.info
Spanish Forum Org
www.spanishforumorg.com
Sur
www.surinenglish.com
Think Spain
www.thinkspain.com
This is Costa Blanca
www.thisiscostablanca.com
TuSpain
www.tuspain.com
Typically Spanish
www.typicallyspanish.com

TRAVEL TO SPAIN
AA
www.theaa.com
Aer Lingus
www.aerlingus.com
Air Scotland
www.air-scotland.com
Avro
www.avro.co.uk
BA
www.ba.com
BMI
www.flybmi.com
Brittany Ferries

www.brittanyferries.com
EasyJet
www.easyjet.com
Eurolines
www.eurolines.co.uk
Eurostar
www.eurostar.co.uk
Excel
www.excelairways.com
Flybe
www.flybe.com
Globespan
www.flyglobespan.com
Iberia Airlines
www.iberiaairlines.co.uk
Jet2
www.jet2.com
Monarch
www.flymonarch.com
MyTravelLite
www.mytravellite.com
P&O
www.poferries.com
RAC
www.rac.co.uk
RailEurope
www.raileurope.co.uk
Renfe
www.renfe.es
Ryanair
www.ryanair.com
Thomsonfly
www.thomsonfly.com
Travelling in Spain
www.travellinginspain.com

SPANISH LIFESTYLE
*A Place in the Sun's everything
Spain* magazine is published
every four weeks
www.everythingspainmag.co.uk

A Place in the Sun Live!
property, travel and lifestyle
exhibition is held twice a year
www.aplaceinthesunlive.com

INDEX

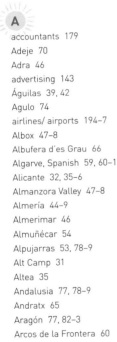